P9-DUS-716

Spoken French

FOR STUDENTS AND TRAVELERS

By CHARLES E. KANY
and MATHURIN DONDO
UNIVERSITY OF CALIFORNIA

D. C. HEATH AND COMPANY
Boston

Printed in the United States of America. (5A9)

PREFACE

The purpose of this book is to offer easy but adequate conversational French to students of the language and to travelers and tourists in France. The book may be considered a basic conversational text not only for beginners with no knowledge of French, but also for those who already possess a foundation. A skeleton grammar is appended for the benefit of those who may wish to consult it. To this end footnoted references will be found throughout the text corresponding to explanatory paragraphs in the Appendix.

The dialogues have been carefully selected to meet the ordinary requirements of the traveler in his daily life and have likewise been graded as to difficulty of expression. Pronunciation has been added in phonetic script for the first part, but not for the second, since at that stage it was no longer felt to be necessary. The usage indicated is that of the cultured Frenchman in ordinary conversation.

The English translation given for each French sentence is a time-saving device particularly helpful for self-instruction.

Class procedure may vary. The most successful methods seem to include some or the majority of the following steps: 1. Teacher answers questions pupils may have on the selection studied. The meaning of every sentence should be clear to all. 2. Books open. Teacher reads aloud. Pupils repeat in chorus sentence by sentence. If these

are too long, they may be divided. 3. Books closed. Teacher reads complete dialogue to class, focusing attention on intonation, facial expression, gestures and action (whenever this can be done). Pupils listen and observe. 4. Books closed. Teacher reads again. Pupils repeat in chorus sentence by sentence. 5. Teacher reads. At end of each sentence or speech he calls on individual pupils (in prearranged order, or by pointing, to save time): the first repeats the sentence in French, the second gives the English meaning so that all can hear it, then the class repeats the sentence in chorus. 6. Books open. Half the class (or the boys) reads one part, the other half (or the girls) reads the second part. 7. Books closed. Students pair off simultaneously. Teacher writes on board key words of dialogue. Pupils begin the dialogue. Then key words are erased and pupils (still in pairs) make variations of their own. 8. Pupils (at first in pairs) improvise a dialogue of similar nature, using additional vocabulary given in notes, etc. Teacher listens, corrects, and answers questions.

After this, if composition is required, pupils may prepare a similar dialogue with variations. These compositions are to be corrected and returned. Furthermore, the teacher may formulate his own questions in French concerning the material under study. Again, each pupil may memorize a few dialogues that appeal to him most. Any two students who have thus selected the same dialogue should then recite it together before the class, with appropriate action and gestures.

C. E. K.
M. D.

CONTENTS

PART II

PRONUNCIATION

The *approximate* English equivalents of the phonetic symbols are as follows:

[i] as in pol*i*ce
[e] " " g*a*te
[ɛ] " " m*e*t
[a] " " p*a*t
[ɑ] " " f*a*ther
[ɔ] " " cl*o*th
[o] " " v*o*te
[u] " " b*oo*t

[k] as in *c*at
[g] " " *go*
[s] " " *so*
[z] " " *z*ero
[ʃ] " " *sh*e
[ʒ] " " a*z*ure
[ɲ] only approximately like o*ni*on, with greater contact area of tongue and palate and less *i*.

[y] no equivalent. Round lips as for [u] and try to pronounce [i].

[ø] no equivalent. Round lips as for [o] and try to pronounce [e].

[œ] no equivalent. Round lips as for [ɔ] and try to pronounce [ɛ].

[r] may be uvular or lingual. In the lingual *r* the tip of tongue vibrates against hard palate. In the uvular *r* (standard among cultivated French) the uvula vibrates against the back of the tongue.

[ə] as in sof*a*, but with lips rounded.

[ɛ̃] is nasalized [ɛ]
[ɑ̃] " " [ɑ]
[ɔ̃] " " [ɔ]
[œ̃] " " [œ]

Allow breath to pass through mouth and nasal passages at same time.

[j] — as in *yes*
[ɥ] — like [y] pronounced rapidly

The following symbols are pronounced approximately as in English: [w], [p], [t], [d], [f], [v], [m], [n], [l].

Sounds enclosed in parentheses are generally pronounced in slow, careful speech, and generally omitted in rapid, familiar speech: **Je vais aller en France** [ʒ(ə) vɛ(z) ale ɑ̃ frɑ̃ːs], *I am going to France.*

No attempt has been made to group the phonetic symbols. Closely related words should be read as a unit.

PART I

SALUTATIONS

Greetings

1. — Bonjour,[1] mademoiselle.[2]
bɔ̃ʒuːr, madmwazɛl.
Good morning, (Miss).
2. — Bonjour, monsieur.
bɔ̃ʒuːr, məsjø.
Good morning, (sir).
3. — Comment allez-vous?[3]
kɔmɑ̃t‿ ale vu?
How are you (lit. 'how go you')?
4. — Bien, merci. Et vous?
bjɛ̃, mɛrsi. e vu?
Well, thank you. And you?
5. — Très bien.
trɛ bjɛ̃.
Very well.
6. — Au revoir,[4] monsieur.
o r(ə)vwaːr, məsjø.
Good-bye, (sir).
7. — Au revoir, mademoiselle.
o r(ə)vwaːr, madmwazɛl.
Good-bye, (Miss).

[1] **bonjour** (lit. 'good day') is used from morning until evening: *good morning, good afternoon, how do you do,* etc.; **bonsoir,** *good evening, good night.* [2] The name of the person addressed is usually omitted in direct speech; the use of **monsieur, madame, mademoi-**

1

1. — **Bonsoir, monsieur Dupont.**
bɔ̃swaːr, məsjø dypɔ̃.
Good evening, Mr. Dupont.
2. — **Bonsoir, madame.**
bɔ̃swaːr, madam.
Good evening, (madame, Mrs.).
3. — **Madame Dupont va bien?**
madam dypɔ̃ va bjɛ̃?
Is Mrs. Dupont well (lit. 'Mrs. Dupont goes well')?
4. — **Oui, merci. Elle va très bien.**
wi, mɛrsi. ɛl va trɛ bjɛ̃.
Yes, thank you. She is very well.
5. — **Et comment va Jean?**
e kɔmɑ̃ va ʒɑ̃?
And how is John?
6. — **Il va bien aussi.**
i(l) va bjɛ̃ osi.
He is well too.
7. — **Alors tout va bien.**
alɔr tu va bjɛ̃.
Then everything is fine (lit. 'all goes well').

selle is the rule. [3] Interrogative form, § 23*b*; the verb **aller,** *to go,* § 40. [4] **au revoir,** *good-bye* (lit. 'to the seeing again)'; **au,** § 2.

PARLEZ-VOUS FRANÇAIS?

Do You Speak French?

1. — Bonjour.
   bõʒuːr.
   How do you do.
2. — Bonjour, monsieur.
   bõʒuːr, məsjø.
   How do you do, (sir).
3. — Vous êtes français?[1]
   vuz‿ ɛt frɑ̃sɛ?
   Are you French?
4. — Oui, monsieur. Et vous?
   wi, məsjø. e vu?
   Yes, sir. And you?
5. — Moi,[2] je suis américain.[3]
   mwa, ʒ(ə) sɥi(z) amerikɛ̃.
   I'm (an) American.
6. — Parlez-vous français?
   parle vu frɑ̃sɛ?
   Do you speak French?
7. — Oui, je parle un peu.
   wi, ʒ(ə) parl œ̃ pø.
   Yes, I speak a little.

[1] Interrogative form, § 23*b*. [2] In conversation the subject pronoun is often doubled. [3] The adjective agrees with the person qualified, § 6. A woman says **je suis américaine** [amerikɛn], **française** [frɑ̃sɛːz], **russe** [rys], *Russian*, etc. [4] Negative form, § 17. [5] Disjunctive form, § 22.

8. — **Vous parlez anglais.**
vu parle ɑ̃glɛ.
You speak English.

9. — **Oui. Et vous, vous parlez anglais?**
wi. e vu vu parle ɑ̃glɛ?
Yes. And you, do you speak English?

10. — **Non, je ne parle pas anglais.**[4]
nɔ̃, ʒə n parl pɑ ɑ̃glɛ.
No, I don't speak English.

11. — **Je regrette.**
ʒə r(ə)grɛt.
I'm sorry.

12. — **Moi**[5] **aussi.**
mwa osi.
I (am), too.

13. — **Au revoir, monsieur.**
o r(ə)vwaːr, məsjø.
Good-bye, (sir).

14. — **Bonjour, monsieur.**
bɔ̃ʒuːr, məsjø.
Good day, (sir).

Repeat the dialogue using other adjectives of nationality: **anglais, anglaise** [ɑ̃glɛ, ɑ̃glɛːz], *English;* **espagnol, espagnole** [ɛspaɲɔl for both], *Spanish;* **italien, italienne** [italjɛ̃, italjɛn], *Italian;* **russe** [rys], *Russian* (*m. and f.*); **allemand, allemande** [almɑ̃, almɑ̃ːd], *German*, etc.

COMPRENEZ-VOUS?

Do You Understand?

1. — Bonsoir, monsieur.
bɔ̃swaːr, məsjø.
Good evening, (sir).

2. — Bonsoir.
bɔ̃swaːr.
Good evening.

3. — Pardon. Avez-vous une [1] allumette?
pardɔ̃. ave vu yn alymɛt?
Pardon me. Have you a match?

4. — Je ne comprends [2] pas. Parlez lentement.
ʒə n kɔ̃prɑ̃ pɑ. parle lɑ̃ːtmɑ̃.
I don't understand. Speak slowly.

5. — Allumette . . . cigarette? Comprenez-vous?
alymɛt . . . sigarɛt? kɔ̃prəne vu?
Match . . . cigarette? Do you understand?

6. — Ah, oui. Je comprends. Voilà,[3] monsieur.
ɑ, wi. ʒ(ə) kɔ̃prɑ̃. vwala, məsjø.
Oh, yes. I understand. There you are, (sir).

7. — Merci bien.
mɛrsi bjɛ̃.
Thank you (very much).

[1] Definite and indefinite articles, §§ 2, 3, 4. [2] Present tense of **comprendre,** § 35, III. [3] **voilà,** *there you are, there is, there are* (lit. 'see there'); **voici,** *here you are, here is, here are* (lit. 'see here'). [4] **il n'y a pas de quoi,** lit. 'there is nothing for which (to thank).'

8. — Il n'y a pas de quoi.[4]
i(l) n j a pɑ t kwa.
You're welcome (or *Don't mention it*).
9. — Pardon. Avez-vous une cigarette?
pardɔ̃. ave vu yn sigarɛt?
Pardon me. Have you a cigarette?
10. — Non, monsieur. Je regrette beaucoup.
nɔ̃, məsjø. ʒə r(ə)grɛt boku.
No, (sir). I am very sorry.
11. — Moi aussi. Voici [3] l'allumette.
mwa osi. vwasi l alymɛt.
So am I. Here's the match.
12. — Merci bien, monsieur.
mɛrsi bjɛ̃, məsjø.
Thank you, (sir).
13. — Il n'y a pas de quoi.
i(l) n j a pɑ t kwa.
Don't mention it.
14. — Au plaisir.[5]
o plɛziːr.
Good-bye.

[5] **au plaisir** = **au plaisir de vous revoir,** lit. 'to the pleasure of seeing you again.'

Repeat the dialogue substituting **un crayon** [œ̃ krɛjɔ̃], *a pencil,* for **une allumette;** and **un morceau de papier** [œ̃ mɔrso d papje], *a piece of paper,* for **une cigarette.**

L'HEURE

The Hour

1. — Quelle heure est-il?
   kɛl œːr ɛt‿il?
   What time is it?
2. — Il est une heure.
   il ɛt‿yn œːr.
   It is one o'clock.
3. — A quelle heure part le train?
   a kɛl œːr paːr lə trɛ̃?
   At what time does the train leave?
4. — A une heure quinze.[1]
   a yn œːr kɛ̃ːz.
   At one fifteen.
5. — A quelle heure part l'avion?
   a kɛl œːr paːr l avjɔ̃?
   At what time does the plane leave?
6. — A une heure trente.[2]
   a yn œːr trɑ̃ːt.
   At one thirty.

[1] **une heure quinze,** *one fifteen* = **une heure un quart** [œ̃ kaːr], *quarter past one.* [2] **une heure trente,** *one thirty* = **une heure et demie** [dmi], *half past one.*

Drill with **trois** [trwɑ], *three,* **quatre** [katr], *four,* **cinq** [sɛ̃ːk], *five,* **six** [sis], *six,* **sept** [sɛt], *seven,* **huit** [ɥit], *eight,* **neuf** [nœf], *nine,* **dix** [dis], *ten,* **onze** [ɔ̃ːz], *eleven,* **douze** [duːz], *twelve* (usually *twelve noon* = **midi** [midi]; *midnight* = **minuit** [minɥi]). Before the word

7. — A quelle heure arrive le train?
a kɛl œːr ariːv lə trɛ̃?
At what time does the train arrive?

8. — A une heure et demie.
a yn œːr e dmi.
At half past one.

9. — A quelle heure arrive le courrier?
a kɛl œːr ariːv lə kurje?
At what times does the mail arrive?

10. — A deux heures moins vingt.
a døz‿œːr mwɛ̃ vɛ̃.
At twenty minutes to two.

11. — Merci bien.
mɛrsi bjɛ̃.
Thank you.

12. — Il n'y a pas de quoi.
i(l) n j a pɑ t kwa.
You're welcome.

heures: [trwɑ] becomes [trwɑz], [sis] becomes [siz], [nœf] becomes [nœv], [dis] becomes [diz].

When indicating the time of trains, buses, theatrical performances, radio programs and all public functions in general, the twenty-four-hour system is used: time is counted from twelve noon to twenty-four (midnight). Thus **quinze heures** (*fifteen o'clock*) = *three* P.M. This official practice, however, is not extended to ordinary conversation.

LE TEMPS

The Weather

1. — Quel temps fait-il [1] aujourd'hui?
kɛl tɑ̃ fɛt‿il oʒurdɥi?
How's the weather?
2. — Il fait très beau.
i(l) fɛ trɛ bo.
It's very fine (weather).
3. — Quelle saison préférez-vous?
kɛl sɛzɔ̃ prefere vu?
What season do you prefer?
4. — Je préfère le printemps.
ʒ(ə) prefɛːr lə prɛ̃tɑ̃.
I prefer spring.
5. — Moi, je préfère l'été.
mwa, ʒ(ə) prefɛːr l ete.
I prefer summer.
6. — En été il fait trop chaud.
ɑ̃n‿ete i(l) fɛ tro ʃo.
In summer it is too hot (warm).
7. — Au printemps il pleut trop.
o prɛ̃tɑ̃ i(l) plø tro.
In spring it rains too much.

[1] **quel temps fait-il?** *how's the weather?* (lit. 'what weather does it make?'): **il fait mauvais** [mɔvɛ] **(temps),** *the weather is bad;* **il fait frais** [frɛ], *it is cool;* **il fait bon** [bɔ̃], *it is nice;* **il fait doux** [du], *it is mild;* **il fait du soleil** [dy sɔlɛːj], *it is sunny;* **il fait clair de lune**

8. — En automne il fait trop de vent.
ãn‿ ɔtɔn i(l) fɛ tro d vã.
In autumn there is too much wind.

9. — En hiver il fait trop froid.
ãn‿ ivɛːr i(l) fɛ tro frwa.
In winter it is too cold.

10. — Je n'aime pas la pluie et la neige.
ʒ(ə) nɛm pɑ la plɥi e la nɛːʒ.
I don't like the rain and the snow.

11. — Aimez-vous la chaleur?
ɛme vu la ʃalœːr?
Do you like the heat?

12. — Oui, mais je n'aime pas le froid.
wi, mɛ ʒ(ə) n ɛm pɑ l frwa.
Yes, but I don't like the cold.

13. — Moi non plus.
mwa nɔ̃ ply.
Neither do I (lit. 'I no more').

14. — Vous êtes comme moi.
vuz‿ ɛt kɔm mwa.
You're like me.

[klɛr də lyn], *it is moonlight;* **il fait glissant** [glisã], *it is slippery;* **il fait du vent** [dy vã], *it is windy;* **il neige** [i nɛːʒ], *it is snowing;* **il gèle** [i ʒɛːl], *it is freezing;* **la tempête** [tãpɛːt], *storm;* **le brouillard** [brujaːr], *fog.*

LA LETTRE

The Letter

1. — Avez-vous une plume et de l'encre? [1]
ave vu(z) yn plym e d(ə) l ɑ̃ːkr?
Have you a pen and (some) ink?
2. — Oui. Pourquoi?
wi. purkwa?
Yes. Why?
3. — Je veux écrire des lettres.
ʒə vø(z) ekriːr de lɛt(r).
I want to write some letters.
4. — J'ai un stylo. Tenez.
ʒ e œ̃ stilo. təne.
I have a fountain pen. Here.
5. — Merci. Vous êtes bien aimable.
mɛrsi. vuz‿ɛt bjɛ̃n‿ɛmabl.
Thank you. You are very kind.
6. — Avez-vous du papier à lettres?
ave vu dy papje a lɛt(r)?
Have you (some) writing paper?
7. — Oui, j'ai du papier et des enveloppes.
wi, ʒ e dy papje e dez‿ɑ̃vlɔp.
Yes, I have paper and envelopes.

[1] Partitive, § 2*i*. [2] The value of the franc as given here is equivalent to two cents, U.S. money. [3] The centime is the hundredth part of a franc; **timbre aéro-postal** [aero pɔstal], *air-mail stamp;* **par avion** [par avjɔ̃], *by air mail.*

8. — Avez-vous des timbres aussi?
ave vu de tɛ̃ːbr osi?
Have you stamps, too?
9. — Ah, non, je n'ai pas de timbres.
ɑ, nɔ̃, ʒ n e pɑ t tɛ̃ːbr.
Oh, no, I haven't any stamps.
10. — Quels timbres voulez-vous?
kɛl tɛ̃ːbr vule vu?
What (kind of) stamps do you want?
11. — Deux à un franc [2] cinquante.[3]
dø a œ̃ frɑ̃ sɛ̃kɑ̃ːt.
Two stamps at one franc fifty.
12. — Tenez. Voilà.
təne. vwala.
Here. There you are.
13. — Vous êtes bien aimable. Merci.
vuz‿ɛt bjɛ̃n‿ɛmabl. mɛrsi.
You're very kind. Thanks.
14. — Il n'y a pas de quoi.
i(l) n j a pɑ t kwa.
Don't mention it.

Practice such phrases as: **Avez-vous du papier? Non, je n'ai pas de papier. Avez-vous des timbres? Non, je n'ai pas de timbres.** Substitute in this same construction all the nouns given so far.

LA FAMILLE

The Family

1. — Vous avez écrit [1] à votre famille?
vuz‿ ave(z)ekri a vɔt(r) famiːj?
Have you written to your family?
2. — Oui, j'ai écrit deux lettres.
wi, ʒ e ekri dø lɛt(r).
Yes, I've written two letters.
3. — A qui avez-vous écrit?
a ki ave vu(z) ekri?
To whom have you written?
4. — A mon père, à ma mère et à Paul.[2]
a mɔ̃ pɛːr, a ma mɛːr e a pɔl.
To my father, to my mother, and to Paul.
5. — Vous écrivez beaucoup de lettres?
vuz‿ ekrive boku d(ə) lɛt(r)?
Do you write many letters?
6. — J'écris souvent à mes parents.[3]
ʒ ekri suvɑ̃ a me parɑ̃.
I write frequently to my parents (or *relatives*).
7. — Où est votre ami Paul à présent?
u ɛ vɔtr ami pɔl a prezɑ̃?
Where is your friend Paul now?

[1] Perfect tense, § 35, II. [2] Possessive adjectives, § 9. [3] **la sœur** [sœːr], *sister;* **l'oncle** [lɔ̃ːkl], *uncle;* **la tante** [tɑ̃ːt], *aunt;* **le cousin** [kuzɛ̃], (*male*) *cousin;* **la cousine** [kuzin], (*female*) *cousin.* [4] **le droit** [drwɑ], *law;* **les langues** [le lɑ̃ːg], *languages.*

8. — Il est à New York.
il ɛ(t) a nœ jɔrk.
He's in New York.

9. — Son frère est à New York aussi?
sɔ̃ frɛːr ɛ(t) a nœ jɔrk osi?
Is his brother in New York, too?

10. — Non, il est en France maintenant.
nɔ̃, il ɛ(t) ɑ̃ frɑ̃s mɛ̃tnɑ̃.
No, he's in France now.

11. — Qu'est-ce que Paul fait à New York?
k ɛ s kə pɔl fɛ a nœ jɔrk?
What is Paul doing in New York?

12. — Il étudie la médecine.[4]
il etydi la medsin.
He is studying medicine.

13. — C'est une profession bien dangereuse.
sɛt‿ yn prɔfɛsjɔ̃ bjɛ̃ dɑ̃ʒrøːz.
That's a dangerous profession.

14. — Pas pour Paul, mais pour ses clients.
pɑ pur pɔl, mɛ pur se kliɑ̃.
Not for Paul, but for his patients (lit. 'clients').

Repeat the dialogue, substituting new nouns: **Oui, j'ai écrit deux lettres** = **Oui, j'ai écrit une carte postale** (*postal card*); **A mon père et à ma mère** = **A ma sœur et à mon oncle; Où est votre ami Paul?** = **Où est votre amie Jeanne? Elle est à Paris,** *etc.*

LA PRÉSENTATION

The Introduction

1. — Qui est cette demoiselle?
ki ɛ sɛt d(ə)mwazɛl?
Who is that young lady?
2. — Suzanne Doré, la fiancée[1] de Paul.
syzan dɔre, la fjɑ̃se d(ə) pɔl.
Susan Doré, Paul's fiancée.
3. — Voulez-vous me présenter?
vule vu m(ə) prezɑ̃te?
Will you introduce me?
4. — Mademoiselle Doré . . . monsieur Blondin.[2]
madmwazɛl dɔre məsjø blɔ̃dɛ̃.
Miss Doré . . . Mr. Blondin.
5. — Monsieur, je suis très heureuse.[3]
məsjø, ʒ(ə) sɥi trɛz‿œrøːz.
(Sir), I am glad (to meet you).
6. — Et moi, mademoiselle, je suis enchanté.
e mwa, madmwazɛl, ʒ(ə) sɥiz‿ɑ̃ʃɑ̃te.
And I'm delighted, Miss Doré.
7. — Vous aimez danser, monsieur?
vuz‿ ɛme dɑ̃se, məsjø?
Do you like to dance, (sir)?

[1] **le fiancé,** *fiancé;* **ils sont fiancés,** *they are engaged;* **les fiançailles** [fjɑ̃sɑːj], *engagement;* **anneau** [ano], *or* **bague** [bag], **de fiançailles,** *engagement ring.* [2] More formally one would say: **Permettez-moi de vous présenter . . .** [pɛrmɛte mwa d(ə) vu prezɑ̃te], *allow me to*

8. — J'adore danser avec une jolie femme.
ʒ adɔːr dɑ̃se avɛk yn ʒɔli fam.
I love to dance with a pretty woman.

9. — Vous êtes galant.
vuz‿ ɛt galɑ̃.
You flatter me (lit. 'you are gallant').

10. — Puis-je avoir [4] la prochaine danse?
pɥi ʒ avwar la prɔʃɛn dɑ̃ːs?
May I have the next dance?

11. — Avec plaisir.
avɛk plɛziːr.
With pleasure.

12. — Merci. Vous êtes trop aimable.
mɛrsi. vuz‿ ɛt trɔp‿ɛmabl.
Thank you. You're very kind.

13. — Cet orchestre vous plaît?
sɛt ɔrkɛstr vu plɛ?
Do you like this orchestra?

14. — Oui, il me plaît beaucoup.
wi, i(l) m(ə) plɛ boku.
Yes, I like it very much.

introduce to you . . . [3] The longer form is: **Je suis très heureux (enchanté) de faire votre connaissance** [də fɛːr vɔtr kɔnɛsɑ̃ːs], *I am very happy (delighted) to make your acquaintance.* [4] **puis-je avoir? = est-ce que je peux avoir?**

C'EST COMBIEN?

How Much Is It?

1. — C'est combien ce [1] chapeau?
   s ɛ kɔ̃bjɛ̃ sə ʃapo?
   How much is that hat?
2. — Ce chapeau-ci ou ce chapeau-là?
   sə ʃapo si u sə ʃapo la?
   This hat (here) or that hat (there)?
3. — Pas celui-là. Celui-ci.
   pɑ səlɥi la. səlɥi si.
   Not that one. This one.
4. — C'est cent francs.
   s ɛ sɑ̃ frɑ̃.
   It's a hundred francs.
5. — C'est cher. Et cette cravate?
   s ɛ ʃɛːr. e sɛt kravat?
   That's expensive. And that necktie?
6. — Cette cravate-ci?
   sɛt kravat si?
   This tie?
7. — Non, pas celle-là. Celle-ci.
   nɔ̃, pɑ sɛl la, sɛl si.
   No, not that one. This one.

[1] Demonstrative adjective, § 14. Practice with these nouns in both singular and plural: **mouchoir** [muʃwaːr], *m. handkerchief;* **bas** [bɑ], *m. stocking;* **complet** [kɔ̃plɛ], *m. suit;* **chemise** [ʃ(ə)miːz], *f. shirt;* **chaussette** [ʃosɛt], *f. sock.* [2] **s.v.p. = s'il vous plaît** [si(l) vu plɛ], *please* (lit. 'if it pleases you'). We abbreviate

8. — Ces cravates sont à vingt francs.
se kravat sɔ̃t‿a vɛ̃ frɑ̃.
These ties are twenty francs apiece.

9. — Donnez-moi celle-ci, s.v.p.[2]
dɔne mwa sɛl si, . . .
Give me this one, please.

10. — Bien. Désirez-vous autre chose?
bjɛ̃. dezire vu ot(r) ʃoːz?
Very well. Do you wish anything else?

11. — C'est combien [3] ces gants?
s ɛ kɔ̃bjɛ̃ se gɑ̃?
How much are these gloves?

12. — Ceux-ci sont à soixante francs.
sø si sɔ̃t‿a swasɑ̃ːt frɑ̃.
These are sixty francs (a pair).

13. — C'est trop cher.[4] Et ceux-là?
s ɛ tro ʃɛːr. e sø la?
That's too dear. And those?

14. — C'est le même prix.
s ɛ l(ə) mɛm pri.
They're the same price.

this phrase to save space. [3] **c'est combien? = combien coûte cela** [kut s(ə)la]? [4] **bon marché** [bɔ̃ marʃe], *cheap;* **articles bon marché** *low-priced goods, bargains;* **une occasion** [ɔkɑzjɔ̃], *bargain;* **livre d'occasion,** *second-hand book.*

VOUS ALLEZ EN FRANCE?[1]

Are You Going to France?

1. — Bonjour, Philippe.
   bɔ̃ʒuːr, filip.
   Good morning, Philip.
2. — Ah, bonjour, René!
   ɑ, bɔ̃ʒuːr, rəne!
   Oh, good morning, René!
3. — Qu'est-ce que vous allez faire cet été?[2]
   k ɛ s kə vuz‿ale fɛːr sɛt‿ete?
   What are you going to do this summer?
4. — Je vais aller en France![2]
   ʒ(ə) vɛ(z) ale ɑ̃ frɑ̃ːs.
   I'm going to France.
5. — Vraiment? Quand partez-vous?
   vrɛmɑ̃? kɑ̃ parte vu?
   Really? When do you leave?
6. — Je pars lundi prochain.[2]
   ʒ(ə) paːr lœ̃di prɔʃɛ̃.
   I leave next Monday.
7. — Pour combien de temps?
   pur kɔ̃bjɛ̃ t tɑ̃?
   For how long?

[1] Interrogative form, § 23*b*. [2] Repeat the dialogue changing **été** to other seasons (**printemps, automne, hiver,** cf. Dialogue 5); **la France** to **l'Angleterre** [lɑ̃glətɛːr], *England,* **l'Italie** [litali], *Italy,* **l'Allemagne** [lalmaɲ], *Germany,* cf. § 2*d*; and **lundi** to other days

8. — **Pour trois mois environ.**
pur trwɑ mwɑ ɑ̃virɔ̃.
For about three months.

9. — **Vous allez rester à Paris?**
vuz‿ ale rɛste a pari?
Will you stay in Paris?

10. — **Deux ou trois semaines seulement.**
dø(z) u trwɑ smɛːn sœlmɑ̃.
Only two or three weeks.

11. — **Vous allez visiter toute l'Europe?**
vuz‿ ale vizite tut lœrɔp?
Are you going to visit all of Europe?

12. — **Oh, non! seulement la France.**
o, nɔ̃! sœlmɑ̃ la frɑ̃ːs.
Oh, no! only France.

13. — **Alors, vous allez faire un beau voyage.**
alɔːr, vuz‿ ale fɛr œ̃ bo vwajaːʒ.
Then you're going to have a beautiful trip.

14. — **J'espère que oui.**
ʒ ɛspɛːr kə wi.
I hope so.

of the week. The days of the week are: **lundi** [lœ̃di], *Monday;* **mardi** [mardi], *Tuesday;* **mercredi** [mɛrkrədi], *Wednesday;* **jeudi** [ʒœdi], *Thursday;* **vendredi** [vɑ̃drədi], *Friday;* **samedi** [samdi], *Saturday;* **dimanche** [dimɑ̃ːʃ], *Sunday.*

POUR RÉSERVER UN PASSAGE

Reserving Passage

1. — Quand part le bateau pour le Havre?
kɑ̃ paːr lə bato pur lə aːv(r)?
When does the boat leave for Le Havre?
2. — Le « Champlain » part le vingt-sept juin.[1]
lə ʃɑ̃plɛ̃ paːr lə vɛ̃t sɛt ʒɥɛ̃ (*or* ʒwɛ̃)
The "Champlain" leaves June 27th.
3. — Réservez-moi un passage, s.v.p.
rezɛrve mwa œ̃ pɑsaːʒ, . . .
Will you reserve passage for me, please?
4. — En première classe?
ɑ̃ prəmjɛːr klɑːs?
In first class?
5. — Non, deuxième classe ou touriste.
nɔ̃, døzjɛm klɑːs u turist.
No, second class or tourist.
6. — Je n'ai plus rien en touriste.
ʒ(ə) n e ply rjɛ̃ ɑ̃ turist.
I have nothing left in tourist.
7. — Et en deuxième?
e ɑ̃ døzjɛm?
And in second?
8. — Il me reste encore une couchette.
i(l) m(ə) rɛst ɑ̃kɔːr yn kuʃɛt.
I have one berth left.

[1] The months are: **janvier** [ʒɑ̃vje], *January;* **février** [fevrie], *February;* **mars** [mars], *March;* **avril** [avril], *April;* **mai** [mɛ], *May;* **juin** [ʒɥɛ̃ or ʒwɛ̃], *June;* **juillet** [ʒɥijɛ], *July;* **août** [u], *August;*

9. — Sur quel pont?
syr kɛl pɔ̃?
On what deck?

10. — Sur le pont C, dans la cabine quinze.
syr l(ə) pɔ̃ se, dɑ̃ la kabin kɛ̃ːz.
On C deck, in Cabin Fifteen.

11. — Montrez-moi le plan du bateau, s.v.p.
mɔ̃tre mwa l(ə) plɑ̃ dy bato, . . .
Please show me the plan of the ship.

12. — Certainement. Le voilà.
sɛrtɛnmɑ̃. lə vwala.
Certainly. Here it is.

13. — Combien coûte le passage en deuxième?
kɔ̃bjɛ̃ kut lə pɑsaːʒ ɑ̃ døzjɛm?
How much does passage cost in second?

14. — Cent cinquante dollars.
sɑ̃ sɛ̃kɑ̃ːt dɔlaːr.
A hundred and fifty dollars.

15. — Bien. Réservez-moi cette couchette.
bjɛ̃. rezɛrve mwa sɛt kuʃɛt.
All right. Reserve that berth for me.

16. — Bien, monsieur. Bonjour, monsieur.
bjɛ̃, məsjø. bɔ̃ʒuːr, məsjø.
Very well, sir. Good-bye (sir).

septembre [sɛptɑ̃ːbr], *September;* **octobre** [ɔktɔːbr], *October;* **novembre** [nɔvɑ̃ːbr], *November;* **décembre** [desɑ̃ːbr], *December.*

Repeat the dialogue changing all numerals; cf. § 31.

AU CONSULAT

At the Consulate

1. — Monsieur le consul de France?
məsjø lə kɔ̃syl d(ə) frɑ̃ːs?
Pardon me, are you the French consul?
2. — Oui, monsieur.
wi, məsjø.
Yes, sir.
3. — Bonjour, monsieur le consul.
bɔ̃ʒuːr, məsjø l(ə) kɔ̃syl.
Good morning, sir.
4. — Bonjour, monsieur.
bɔ̃ʒuːr, məsjø.
Good morning, (sir).
5. — Voulez-vous viser mon passeport, s.v.p.?
vule vu vize mɔ̃ pɑspɔːr, . . .
Will you please visa my passport?
6. — Vous avez les documents nécessaires?
vuz‿ ave le dɔkymɑ̃ nesesɛːr?
Have you the necessary documents?
7. — Deux photos et l'extrait de naissance.[1]
dø fɔto e l ɛkstrɛ d(ə) nɛsɑ̃ːs.
Two photographs and my birth certificate.

[1] **le certificat de bonne conduite** [sɛrtifika də bɔn kɔ̃dɥit], *good conduct (character) certificate;* **certificat de santé** [sɑ̃te], *health certificate;* **vaccination** [vaksinasjɔ̃], *vaccination;* **vacciner** [vaksine],

8. — Montrez-les-moi, je vous prie.
mɔ̃tre le mwa, ʒ(ə) vu pri.
May I see them? (lit. 'show them to me, I beg you.')

9. — Voilà, monsieur.
vwala, məsjø.
Here they are, sir.

10. — Vous êtes citoyen américain? [2]
vuz‿ ɛt sitwajɛ̃ amerikɛ̃?
Are you an American citizen?

11. — Oui, monsieur. Je suis né [3] à Chicago.
wi, məsjø. ʒə sɥi ne a ʃikago.
Yes, sir. I was born in Chicago.

12. — Voilà. Votre passeport est visé.
vwala. vot(r) pɑspɔːr ɛ vize.
There you are. Your passport is visaed.

13. — C'est combien, je vous prie?
s ɛ kɔ̃bjɛ̃, ʒ(ə) vu pri?
How much is it, please?

14. — C'est dix dollars.
s ɛ di dɔlaːr.
It's ten dollars.

to vaccinate; **se faire vacciner,** *to get vaccinated.* [2] **citoyen américain** *m.*, **citoyenne américaine** [sitwajɛn amerikɛn] *f.* [3] **je suis né** [ne] *m.*, **je suis née** [ne] *f.*

LE BILLET DE PASSAGE

The Steamship Ticket

1. — Vous avez mon billet de passage?
vuz‿ ave mɔ̃ bijɛ d(ə) pɑsaːʒ?
Have you my ticket?
2. — Tout est prêt. Et votre passeport?
tut‿ ɛ prɛ. e vɔt(r) pɑspɔːr?
Everything's ready. And your passport?
3. — Je l'ai. Tout est en règle.
ʒə l e. tut‿ ɛ(t) ɑ̃ rɛgl.
I have it. Everything is in order.
4. — Voici votre billet et des étiquettes.
vwasi vɔt(r) bijɛ e dez‿etikɛt.
Here are your ticket and some labels.
5. — Pourquoi toutes ces étiquettes?
purkwa tut sez‿etikɛt?
Why all these labels?
6. — C'est pour vos bagages.
s ɛ pur vo bagaːʒ.
For your baggage.
7. — Ah! Pour ma malle et pour ma valise.
ɑ! pur ma mal e pur ma valiːz.
Oh! For my trunk and my suitcase.
8. — C'est ça. Mettez-y votre adresse.
s ɛ sa. mɛtez‿ i vɔtr adrɛs.
That's right. Put your address on them.

9. — Bien. A quelle heure part le bateau?
bjɛ̃. a kɛl œːr paːr lə bato?
All right. What time does the boat leave?

10. — A vingt-trois heures.
a vɛ̃t trwɑz‿œːr.
At eleven P.M. (lit. 'at 23 o'clock').

11. — Et à quelle heure peut-on aller à bord?
e a kɛl œːr pøt‿ɔ̃ ale a bɔːr?
And at what time may one go aboard?

12. — Après déjeuner.
aprɛ deʒœne.
After lunch.

13. — Merci, monsieur. Au revoir.
mɛrsi, məsjø. o r(ə)vwaːr.
Thank you, (sir). Good-bye.

14. — Mais vous n'avez pas payé le billet!
mɛ vu n ave pɑ peje l(ə) bijɛ!
But you haven't paid for your ticket!

15. — Pardon. Je suis tellement ému.
pardɔ̃. ʒ(ə) sɥi tɛlmɑ̃(t) emy.
Pardon me. I'm so excited.

16. — Merci, monsieur. Bon voyage!
mɛrsi, məsjø. bɔ̃ vwajaːʒ!
Thank you, sir. Bon voyage!

LA TRAVERSÉE

The Crossing

1. — Permettez-moi de me présenter: —
pɛrmɛte mwa də m(ə) prezɑ̃te: —
Allow me to introduce myself: —

2. — Moi, je m'appelle —
mwa, ʒ(ə) m apɛl —
My name is —

3. — C'est votre première traversée?
s ɛ vɔt(r) prəmjɛːr travɛrse?
Is it your first crossing?

4. — Oui. Pour vous aussi?
wi. pur vu osi?
Yes. For you too?

5. — Moi, je vais tous les ans[1] en Europe.
mwa, ʒ(ə) vɛ tu lez‿ɑ̃ ɑ̃n‿œrɔp.
I go to Europe every year.

6. — Vous aimez voyager en bateau?
vuz‿ eme vwajaʒe ɑ̃ bato?
Do you like to travel by boat?

7. — Oui, j'aime beaucoup la vie à bord.
wi, ʒ ɛm boku la vi a bɔːr.
Yes, I'm very fond of life aboard (ship).

[1] **an** [ɑ̃] *m.* = **année** [ane] *f. year.* Except in certain locutions such as **tous les ans** [tu lez‿ɑ̃], *every year*, **le nouvel an** [lə nuvɛl ɑ̃], *New Year*, the word **an** is used with a specific number (**quatre ans**

8. — Vous n'avez jamais le mal de mer?
vu n ave ʒamɛ l(ə) mal d(ə) mɛr?
You're never seasick?

9. — Non, jamais, Dieu merci. Et vous?
nɔ̃, ʒamɛ, djø mɛrsi. e vu?
No, never, thank heaven. And you?

10. — Ah! je ne sais pas encore. Attendons.[2]
ɑ! ʒə n(ə) se pɑ(z) ɑ̃kɔːr. atɑ̃dɔ̃.
Oh! I don't know yet. Let's wait.

11. — La mer est calme en cette saison.
la mɛr ɛ kalm ɑ̃ sɛt sɛzɔ̃.
The ocean is calm at this season.

12. — Il n'y a pas de tempête en été?
i(l) n j a pɑ t tɑ̃pɛːt ɑ̃n‿ete?
There are no storms in summer?

13. — Ah! on ne sait jamais.
ɑ! ɔ̃ n(ə) se ʒamɛ.
Oh, one never knows!

14. — J'espère que non.
ʒ ɛspɛr kə nɔ̃.
I hope not.

[katr ɑ̃], **cinq ans** [sɛ̃k ɑ̃]); **année** is used in other cases: **cette année,** *this year;* **l'année prochaine** [prɔʃɛn], *next year;* **l'année passée** [pɑse], *last year.* [2] § 35, III, imperative.

LE MÉDECIN DE BORD

The Ship's Doctor

1. — Bonjour, monsieur le docteur.
bɔ̃ʒuːr, məsjø l(ə) dɔktœːr.
How do you do, doctor.

2. — Bonjour. Comment allez-vous?
bɔ̃ʒuːr. kɔmɑ̃t‿ ale vu?
How do you do. How are you?

3. — Pas très bien, docteur.
pɑ trɛ bjɛ̃, dɔktœːr.
Not very well, (doctor).

4. — Qu'est-ce que vous avez?
k ɛ s kə vuz‿ave?
What's the matter?

5. — J'ai mal à la tête.[1]
ʒ e mal a la tɛːt.
I have a headache.

6. — Vous mangez bien?
vu mɑ̃ʒe bjɛ̃?
Do you eat well?

7. — Non, je mange très peu.
nɔ̃, ʒ(ə) mɑ̃ʒ trɛ pø.
No, I eat very little.

[1] **(avoir) mal à la gorge** [gɔrʒ], *(to have) a sore throat,* **mal à la tête** [tɛːt], *a headache,* **mal aux dents** [dɑ̃], *a toothache,* **mal au doigt** [dwɑ], *a sore finger,* **mal au pied** [pje], *a sore foot,* **le mal du pays** [pe(j)i], *(to be) homesick;* **mes os** [mez‿o] **me font mal,** *my bones*

8. — Avez-vous mal à l'estomac?
ave vu mal a l ɛstɔma?
Does your stomach trouble you?

9. — Oui, l'estomac est très faible.
wi, l ɛstɔma ɛ trɛ fɛːbl.
Yes, my stomach is very weak.

10. — Vous avez le mal de mer, jeune homme.
vuz‿ ave l(ə) mal d(ə) mɛr, jœn ɔm.
You are seasick, young man.

11. — Y a-t-il [2] un remède, docteur?
j a t il œ̃ r(ə)mɛd, dɔktœːr?
Is there any cure for it, doctor?

12. — Oui, il y a un bon remède.
wi, i(l) j a œ̃ bɔ̃ r(ə)mɛd.
Yes, there's a good cure for it.

13. — Faut-il [3] prendre des pilules?
fot‿i(l) prɑ̃ːd(r) de pilyl?
Must I take pills?

14. — Non, il faut [3] descendre à terre.
nɔ̃, i(l) fo desɑ̃ːdr a tɛːr.
No, you must go ashore.

ache; **fièvre** [fjɛːvr], *f. fever;* **je suis enrhumé** [ɑ̃ryme] *or* **j'ai un rhume** [œ̃ rym], *I have a cold.* [2] § 23*d;* **il y a,** *there is, there are.* [3] **il faut,** *it is necessary* (impersonal).

L'ARRIVÉE AU PORT

Arriving at the Port

1. — Quand débarquons-nous?
   kɑ̃ debarkɔ̃ nu?
   When do we go ashore?
2. — Après la visite des passeports.
   aprɛ la vizit de pɑspɔːr.
   After passport inspection.
3. — Est-ce que ça [1] dure longtemps?
   ɛ s kə sa dyːr lɔ̃tɑ̃?
   Does that take a long time?
4. — Une demi-heure (ou trois quarts d'heure).
   yn dəmi œːr (u trwɑ kaːr d œːr).
   Half an hour (or three quarters of an hour).
5. — Et alors on peut [2] descendre à terre?
   e alɔːr ɔ̃ pø desɑ̃ːdr a tɛːr?
   And then may we go ashore?
6. — Certainement. Vos bagages sont prêts?
   sɛrtɛnmɑ̃. vo bagaːʒ sɔ̃ prɛ?
   Certainly. Is your baggage ready?
7. — Voici ma valise. Mais où est ma malle?
   vwasi ma valiːz. mɛ u ɛ ma mal?
   Here is my suitcase. But where's my trunk?
8. — Votre malle est déjà sur le quai.
   vɔt(r) mal ɛ deʒa syr l(ə) ke.
   Your trunk is already on the dock.

[1] **ça = cela.** [2] From **pouvoir,** § 40. [3] Reflexive imperative, § 37, I.

9. — Nous partons aussitôt pour Paris?
nu partɔ̃ osito pur pari?
Do we leave immediately for Paris?

10. — Oui, après la visite de la douane.
wi, aprɛ la vizit d(ə) la dwan.
Yes, after customs inspection.

11. — Où prend-on le train?
u prɑ̃ːt‿ɔ̃ l(ə) trɛ̃?
Where does one take the train?

12. — Le train vient tout près du bateau.
lə trɛ̃ vjɛ̃ tu prɛ dy bato.
The train comes right up to the boat.

13. — C'est un train rapide?
s ɛt‿œ̃ trɛ̃ rapid?
Is it an express?

14. — Évidemment.
evidamɑ̃.
Of course.

15. — Eh bien, au revoir.
e bjɛ̃, o r(ə)vwaːr.
Well, good-bye.

16. — Au revoir. Amusez-vous[3] bien.
o r(ə)vwaːr. amyze vu bjɛ̃.
Good-bye. Have a good time.

LA VISITE DE LA DOUANE

The Customs Inspection

1. — Vous n'avez rien à déclarer?
vu n ave rjɛ̃(n) a deklare?
You haven't anything to declare?
2. — Non, monsieur, je ne crois pas.[1]
nɔ̃, məsjø, ʒə n(ə) krwɑ pɑ.
No, sir, I think not.
3. — Avez-vous du tabac?
ave vu dy taba?
Have you any tobacco?
4. — J'ai seulement un paquet de cigarettes.
ʒ e sœlmɑ̃ œ̃ pakɛ d(ə) sigarɛt.
I have only one package of cigarettes.
5. — Ouvrez votre valise . . .
uvre vɔt(r) valiːz . . .
Open your suitcase . . .
6. — Ça, c'est un carton de cigarettes.
sa s ɛt‿œ̃ kartɔ̃ d(ə) sigarɛt.
That's a carton of cigarettes.
7. — Combien y a-t-il là-dedans?
kɔ̃bjɛ̃ j a t i(l) la d‿dɑ̃?
How many does it contain?
8. — Il y a dix paquets de vingt.
i(l) j a di pakɛ d(ə) vɛ̃.
There are ten packages of twenty (each).

[1] **je ne crois pas = je crois que non.**

9. — Et vous comptez les vendre?
e vu kɔ̃te le vɑ̃ːdr?
And do you intend to sell them?

10. — Non, monsieur; je compte les fumer.
nɔ̃, məsjø; ʒ(ə) kɔ̃t le fyme.
No, sir; I intend to smoke them.

11. — Qu'est-ce qu'il y a dans votre malle?
k ɛ s k i(l) j a dɑ̃ vɔt(r) mal?
What is there in your trunk?

12. — Des vêtements et quelques livres.
de vɛtmɑ̃ e kɛlkə liːvr.
Clothes and some books.

13. — Rien que des objets personnels?
rjɛ̃ kə dez‿ɔbʒɛ pɛrsɔnɛl?
Only articles for your personal use?

14. — Non, rien. Faut-il ouvrir?
nɔ̃, rjɛ̃. fot‿i(l) uvriːr?
Nothing else. Must I open it?

15. — Ce n'est pas la peine d'ouvrir.
s(ə) n ɛ pɑ la pɛn d uvriːr.
Don't bother to open it.

16. — Merci bien, monsieur.
mɛrsi bjɛ̃, məsjø.
Thank you, sir.

DANS LE TRAIN

In the Train

1. — Pardon. Cette place est occupée ?
pardɔ̃. sɛt plas ɛt‿ɔkype?
Pardon me. Is this seat taken?
2. — Non, monsieur, elle est libre.
nɔ̃, məsjø, ɛl ɛ liːbr.
No, (sir), it's unoccupied.
3. — C'est bien le train pour Paris ?
s ɛ bjɛ̃ l(ə) trɛ̃ pur pari?
Is this the right train for Paris?
4. — Oui, c'est l'express pour Paris.
wi, s ɛ l ɛksprɛs pur pari.
Yes, it's the express train to Paris.
5. — Peut-on fumer dans ce compartiment ?
pøt‿ɔ̃ fyme dɑ̃ sə kɔ̃partimɑ̃?
Is smoking allowed in this compartment?
6. — Il n'est pas défendu de fumer.
i(l) n ɛ pɑ defɑ̃dy d(ə) fyme.
Smoking is not forbidden.
7. — La fumée ne vous gêne pas, madame ?
la fyme nə vu ʒɛːn pɑ, madam?
The smoke doesn't bother you, madam?
8. — Pas du tout, monsieur. Au contraire.
pɑ dy tu, məsjø. o kɔ̃trɛːr.
Not at all, (sir). On the contrary.

9. — Ah, voilà le contrôleur qui vient.
α, vwala l(ə) kɔ̃trolœːr ki vjɛ̃.
Oh, here comes the conductor.

10. — Vos billets, s.v.p.!
vo bijɛ, . . .
Your tickets, please!

11. — Voici mon bulletin de bagages.
vwasi mɔ̃ byltɛ̃ d(ə) bagaːʒ.
Here's my baggage check.

12. — Votre billet de chemin de fer?
vɔt(r) bijɛ d(ə) ʃmɛ̃ d(ə) fɛːr?
Your railroad ticket?

13. — Est-ce que je l'ai perdu?
ɛ s kə ʒ(ə) l e pɛrdy?
Have I lost it?

14. — Le voilà sur le plancher.
lə vwala syr lə plɑ̃ʃe.
There it is on the floor.

15. — Oh, comme je suis bête!
o, kɔm ʒ(ə) sɥi bɛːt!
Oh, how stupid I am!

16. — Montrez-le à la gare.
mɔ̃tre lə a la gaːr.
Show it at the station.

L'ARRIVÉE A PARIS

Arriving in Paris

1. — Facteur!
faktœːr!
Porter!
2. — Donnez-moi votre valise, monsieur.
dɔne mwa vɔt(r) valiːz, məsjø.
Give me your suitcase, sir.
3. — Allez prendre ma malle, s.v.p.
ale prɑ̃ːd(r) ma mal, . . .
Please go and get my trunk.
4. — Oui, monsieur. Votre bulletin?
wi, məsjø. vɔt(r) byltɛ̃?
Yes, sir. Your check?
5. — Le voilà.
lə vwala.
Here it is.
6. — Bon. Je vais chercher votre malle.
bɔ̃. ʒ(ə) vɛ ʃɛrʃe vɔt(r) mal.
Fine. I'll go and get your trunk.
7. — Vous allez à la salle des bagages?
vuz‿ale a la sal de bagaːʒ?
Are you going to the baggage room?

[1] **à l'entrée** [a lɑ̃tre], *at the entrance.* [2] Reflexive imperatives, § 37, I. Some common phrases with the imperative: **soyez tranquille** [swaje trɑ̃kil], *set your mind at rest, don't worry;* **laissez-moi** [lɛse-mwa] **tranquille,** *leave me alone;* **soyez le bienvenu** [bjɛ̃vny],

8. — Oui. Attendez-moi un instant.
wi. atãde mwa œ̃n‿ɛ̃stã.
Yes. Wait a minute for me.

9. — Sur le quai ou dans la salle d'attente?
syr lə ke u dã la sal d atãːt?
On the platform or in the waiting room?

10. — Attendez-moi là-bas, à la sortie.[1]
atãde mwa la bɑ, a la sɔrti.
Wait for me down there, at the exit.

11. — Bien. Dépêchez-vous,[2] n'est-ce pas?
bjɛ̃. depɛʃe vu n ɛ s pɑ?
All right. Hurry, won't you?

12. — Oui, oui. Ne vous inquiétez pas.[2]
wi, wi. nə vuz‿ɛ̃kjete pɑ.
Yes, yes. Don't worry.

13. — Ah, voilà ma malle. Appelez un taxi.
ɑ, vwala ma mal. aple(z) œ̃ taksi.
Oh, there's my trunk. Call a taxi.

14. — Oui, monsieur. Tout de suite.
wi, məsjø. tu t sɥit.
Yes, sir. Right away.

la bienvenue [bjɛ̃vny], *welcome!* **ayez la bonté de me faire savoir** [ɛje la bɔ̃te d(ə) m(ə) fɛːr savwaːr], *please let me know;* **veuillez** [vøje] **bien me dire l'heure,** *please tell me the time.*

LE TAXI

The Taxi

1. — Taxi? Chauffeur, vous êtes libre?
   taksi? ʃofœːr, vuz‿ɛt liːbr?
   Taxi? Driver, are you free?
2. — Oui, monsieur. Montez.
   wi, məsjø. mɔ̃te.
   Yes, sir. Get in.
3. — Rue Jacob, numéro 15 (quinze).
   ry ʒakɔb, nymero kɛ̃ːz.
   15 Jacob Street.
4. — Oui, monsieur.
   wi, məsjø.
   Yes, sir.
5. — C'est loin d'ici, la rue Jacob?
   s ɛ lwɛ̃ d isi, la ry ʒakɔb?
   Is Jacob Street far from here?
6. — Pas très loin.
   pɑ trɛ lwɛ̃.
   Not very far.
7. — Et ça, c'est la Seine?
   e sa, s ɛ la sɛn?
   And is that the Seine?
8. — Oui. Nous allons traverser ce pont.
   wi. nuz‿alɔ̃ travɛrse s(ə) pɔ̃.
   Yes. We are going to cross that bridge.

9. — La circulation est intense.
la sirkylasjɔ̃ ɛt‿ɛ̃tɑ̃ːs.
Traffic is heavy.

10. — Oui, et puis il y a trop d'agents.
wi, e pɥi i(l) j a tro d aʒɑ̃.
Yes, and there are too many "cops."

11. — N'allez pas si vite!
n ale pɑ si vit!
Don't go so fast!

12. — Voilà votre hôtel.
vwala vɔtr otɛl.
There's your hotel.

13. — Nous voilà arrivés! C'est combien?
nu vwala arive! s ɛ kɔ̃bjɛ̃?
Here we are! How much is it?

14. — Le prix est indiqué au compteur.
lə pri ɛt‿ɛ̃dike o kɔ̃tœːr.
The fare is shown on the meter.

15. — Voilà. Gardez la monnaie.
vwala. garde la mɔnɛ.
Here you are. Keep the change.

16. — Merci, monsieur.
mɛrsi, məsjø.
Thank you, sir.

A L'HÔTEL (*a*)

At the Hotel (a)

1. — Bonjour, monsieur. Vous désirez?
   bɔ̃ʒuːr, məsjø. vu dezire?
   How do you do, sir. What did you wish?
2. — Une chambre [1] pour une personne, s.v.p.
   yn ʃɑ̃ːbr pur yn pɛrsɔn, . . .
   A single room, please.
3. — Nous en avons une au troisième.
   nuz ɑ̃n avɔ̃(z) yn o trwɑzjɛm.
   We have one on the third floor.
4. — Elle donne sur la cour ou sur la rue?
   ɛl dɔn syr la kuːr u syr la ry?
   Does it look out on the court or on the street?
5. — Sur la rue. Avec eau chaude et froide.
   syr la ry. avɛk o ʃod e frwad.
   On the street. With hot and cold water.
6. — Est-ce que je peux voir la chambre?
   ɛ s kə ʒ(ə) pø vwaːr la ʃɑ̃ːbr?
   May I see the room?
7. — Par ici. Voici l'ascenseur.
   par isi. vwasi l asɑ̃sœːr.
   This way. Here's the elevator.

[1] **une chambre pour deux** [pur dø], *double room;* **un appartement à trois pièces** [œ̃n‿apartəmɑ̃ a trwɑ pjɛs], *three-room apartment;* **meublé** [mœble], *furnished;* **non meublé,** *unfurnished;* **le lit** [li], *bed;* **la chaise** [ʃɛːz], *chair;* **une armoire** [armwaːr], *clothes closet.*

8\. — C'est combien, cette chambre?
s ɛ kɔ̃bjɛ̃, sɛt ʃɑ̃ːbr?
How much is this room?

9\. — Trente-cinq francs par jour.[2]
trɑ̃t sɛ̃ frɑ̃ par ʒuːr.
Thirty-five francs a day.

10\. — Et par semaine? [2]
e par s(ə)mɛn?
And by the week?

11\. — C'est deux cents francs.
s ɛ dø sɑ̃ frɑ̃.
It's two hundred francs.

12\. — Bon, je prends cette chambre.
bɔ̃, ʒə prɑ̃ sɛt ʃɑ̃ːbr.
All right. I'll take this room.

13\. — Le garçon va monter vos bagages.
lə garsɔ̃ va mɔ̃te vo bagaːʒ.
The boy will bring up your baggage.

14\. — Merci, monsieur.
mɛrsi, məsjø.
Thank you, sir.

[2] **par jour,** *a day;* **par semaine** [s(ə)mɛn], *a week;* **par mois** [mwɑ], *a month;* **à la journée** [ʒurne], *by the day;* **à la semaine,** *by the week;* **au mois** [o mwɑ], *by the month.*

A L'HÔTEL (*b*)

At the Hotel (*b*)

1. — (*Au téléphone*) [1] Allô! allô!
   (o telefɔn) alo! alo!
   (At the telephone) *Hello! Hello!*
2. — J'écoute. Vous désirez, monsieur?
   ʒ ekut. vu dezire, məsjø?
   Hello (lit. 'I listen'). *What did you wish, sir?*
3. — Du savon et des serviettes,[2] s.v.p.
   dy savɔ̃ e de sɛrvjɛt, ...
   Soap and towels, please.
4. — La bonne va vous les monter.
   la bɔn va vu le mɔ̃te.
   The maid will bring them up to you.
5. — (*La bonne frappe à la porte*) Entrez.
   (la bɔn frap a la pɔrt) ɑ̃tre.
   (The maid knocks at the door) *Come in.*
6. — Voici des serviettes et du savon.
   vwasi de sɛrvjɛt e dy savɔ̃.
   Here are the towels and soap.
7. — Merci, mademoiselle.
   mɛrsi, madmwazɛl.
   Thank you, (Miss).

[1] **raccrocher le récepteur** [rakrɔʃe lə resɛptœːr], *to hang up the receiver;* **décrocher** [dekrɔʃe], *to take down;* **la ligne est occupée** [la liɲ ɛ(t) ɔkype], *the line is busy;* **ici monsieur X,** *Mr. X speaking;* **service interurbain** [sɛrvis ɛ̃tɛryrbɛ̃], *long-distance service.* [2] **ser-**

8. — Avez-vous assez d'une couverture ?[3]
ave vu(z) ase d yn kuvɛrtyr?
Is one blanket enough for you?

9. — Oh, oui, c'est bien assez.
o, wi, s ɛ bjɛ̃n‿ase.
Oh, yes, that's quite enough.

10. — Vous avez tout ce qu'il vous faut ?
vuz‿ave tu s k i(l) vu fo?
Have you everything you need?

11. — Je crois que oui.
ʒ(ə) krwɑ k(ə) wi.
I think so.

12. — Sonnez,[4] s'il vous manque quelque chose.
sɔne, s i(l) vu mɑ̃ːk kɛlkə ʃoːz.
Ring if you need anything.

13. — Merci. Il ne me manque rien.
mɛrsi. i(l) nə mə mɑ̃k rjɛ̃.
Thank you. I don't need anything.

14. — Bonsoir, monsieur.
bɔ̃swaːr, məsjø.
Good night (lit. 'good evening'), *sir.*

viette de bain [də bɛ̃], *bath towel.* [3] **drap** [dra], *m. sheet;* **oreiller** [ɔrɛje], *m. pillow;* **matelas** [matlɑ], *m. mattress.* [4] **la sonnette ne marche pas** [la sɔnɛt nə marʃ pɑ], *the bell is out of order.*

L'AUTOBUS

The Bus

1. — L'autobus s'arrête ici, n'est-ce pas?
l otɔbys s arɛːt isi, n ɛ s pɑ?
The bus stops here, doesn't it?
2. — Quel autobus voulez-vous prendre?
kɛl otɔbys vule vu prɑ̃ːdr?
Which bus do you want to take?
3. — Celui qui va à la Place de l'Opéra.
səlɥi ki va a la plas d(ə) l ɔpera.
The one that goes to the Place de l'Opéra.
4. — Il s'arrête ici. Vous avez un numéro?
i(l) s arɛːt isi. vuz‿ ave(z) œ̃ nymero?
It stops here. Have you a number?
5. — Non. Est-ce que c'est nécessaire?
nɔ̃. ɛ s kə s ɛ nesesɛːr?
No. Is that necessary?
6. — Ah oui, aux heures de presse.
ɑ wi, oz‿ œːr də prɛs.
Oh yes, during rush hours.
7. — Bon. Je vais en[1] prendre un.
bɔ̃. ʒ(ə) vɛ(z) ɑ̃ prɑ̃ːdr œ̃.
All right. I'll take one.

[1] **en,** § 20*b*. [2] **descendre** [desɑ̃ːdr], *to get out* or *off;* **la fin de section** [fɛ̃ də sɛksjɔ̃], *end of zone;* **le terminus** [tɛrminys], *end of the line;* **un carnet de tickets** [karnɛ də tikɛ], *book of tickets;* **détacher** [detaʃe], *to tear off;* **autocar** [otɔkaːr], *m. motor coach,*

8. — Dépêchez-vous! Le voilà qui vient.
depɛʃe vu! lə vwala ki vjɛ̃.
Hurry up! Here it comes.

9. — (*Le conducteur*) Trente, trente et un...
(lə kɔ̃dyktœːr) trɑ̃ːt, trɑ̃t e œ̃...
(The conductor) *Thirty, thirty-one*...

10. — Est-ce que je peux monter?[2]
ɛ s kə ʒ(ə) pø mɔ̃te?
May I get on?

11. — (*Le conducteur*) Trente-deux...
(lə kɔ̃dyktœːr) trɑ̃t dø ...
(The conductor) *Thirty-two*...

12. — Trente-trois. Je peux monter?
trɑ̃t trwɑ. ʒ(ə) pø mɔ̃te?
Thirty-three. May I get on?

13. — Complet! Attendez le suivant.
kɔ̃plɛ! atɑ̃de l(ə) sɥivɑ̃.
Full! Wait for the next one.

14. — J'aime mieux prendre le métro.
ʒ ɛm mjø prɑ̃ːdr lə metro.
I prefer to take the subway.

interurban bus; **le tramway** [tramwɛ], *streetcar;* **le dernier arrêt** [dɛrnje arɛ], *last stop;* **s'arrêter** [sarɛte], *to stop;* **il est défendu de fumer** [il ɛ defɑ̃dy d(ə) fyme], *smoking is not allowed.*

LE MÉTRO

The Subway

1. — Où est la station du métro?
u ɛ la stɑsjɔ̃ dy metro?
Where is the subway station?
2. — Il y en a une boulevard Montparnasse.
i(l) j ɑ̃n‿a yn bulvaːr mɔ̃parnas.
There is one at Boulevard Montparnasse.
3. — Ce n'est pas trop loin?
sə n ɛ pɑ tro lwɛ̃?
It isn't too far?
4. — A deux rues d'ici. J'y vais aussi.
a dø ry d isi. ʒ i vɛ(z) osi.
Two blocks from here. I'm going there too.
5. — Cette ligne va à la Place de l'Opéra?
sɛt liɲ va a la plas d(ə) l ɔpera?
Does that line go to the Place de l'Opéra?
6. — Il faut changer en route.
i(l) fo ʃɑ̃ʒe ɑ̃ rut.
You have to change on the way.
7. — Où faut-il changer?
u fot‿i(l) ʃɑ̃ʒe?
Where must I change?
8. — A la station du Châtelet.
a la stɑsjɔ̃ dy ʃɑtlɛ.
At the Châtelet station.

9. — L'entrée du métro, c'est là-bas?
l ɑ̃tre dy metro, s ɛ la bɑ?
Is the subway entrance down there?

10. — Oui, en face du bureau de tabac.
wi, ɑ̃ fas dy byro t taba.
Yes, opposite the tobacco stand.

11. — Vous avez déjà votre billet?
vuz‿ ave deʒa vɔt(r) bijɛ?
Have you your ticket (already)?

12. — Non, je vais le prendre au guichet.
nɔ̃, ʒ(ə) vɛ l(ə) prɑ̃ːdr o giʃɛ.
No, I'm going to get it at the window.

13. — Vous prenez un billet de première?
vu prəne œ̃ bijɛ d(ə) prəmjɛːr?
Are you going to get a first-class ticket?

14. — Oui. Il y a toujours de la place.
wi. i(l) j a tuʒuːr d(ə) la plas.
Yes. There's always room there.

15. — Vous avez raison.
vuz‿ ave rɛzɔ̃.
You're right.

16. — Dépêchons-nous. Voilà le train.
depɛʃɔ̃ nu. vwala l(ə) trɛ̃.
Let's hurry. There's the train.

AU CAFÉ

At the Café

1. — Vous n'êtes pas fatigué?
vu n ɛt pɑ fatige?
You're not tired?

2. — Si,[1] je suis fatigué et j'ai soif.[2]
si, ʒ(ə) sɥi fatige e ʒ e swaf.
Yes, I'm tired and I'm thirsty.

3. — Moi, je n'ai pas soif, mais j'ai faim.
mwa, ʒ(ə) n e pɑ swaf, mɛ ʒ e fɛ̃.
I'm not thirsty but I'm hungry.

4. — Eh bien, entrons dans ce café.
e bjɛ̃, ɑ̃trɔ̃ dɑ̃ s(ə) kafe.
All right then, let's go into this café.

5. — J'aime mieux m'asseoir sur la terrasse.[3]
ʒ ɛm mjø m aswaːr syr la tɛras.
I prefer to sit outside.

6. — Oui, il fait chaud à l'intérieur.
wi, i(l) fɛ ʃo a l ɛ̃terjœːr.
Yes, it's warm inside.

7. — Asseyons-nous à cette table.
asejɔ̃ nu a sɛt tabl.
Let's sit at that (or *this*) *table.*

[1] After a negative question **si,** *yes,* takes the place of **oui.** [2] lit. 'I have thirst.' [3] That part of a café which is on the sidewalk. [4] **on est très bien,** *one is very comfortable;* **on est mieux ici,** *one is more comfortable here;* **on est mal ici,** *one is uncomfortable here;* **ce**

8. — On est très bien [4] dans ce coin. Garçon!
ɔ̃n‿ɛ trɛ bjɛ̃ dɑ̃ s(ə) kwɛ̃. garsɔ̃!
This is a very comfortable corner. Waiter!

9. — (*Le garçon*) Messieurs?
(lə garsɔ̃) mesjø?
(Waiter) *Gentlemen?*

10. — Moi, je prends une limonade.
mwa, ʒ(ə) prɑ̃ yn limɔnad.
I'll take a lemonade.

11. — Un café pour moi.
œ̃ kafe pur mwa.
A (*cup* or *glass of*) *coffee for me.*

12. — (*Le garçon*) Café crème [5] ou nature?
(lə garsɔ̃) kafe krɛm u natyːr?
(The waiter) *With cream or black?*

13. — Nature. Et un sandwich au jambon.[6]
natyːr. e œ̃ sɑ̃dwitʃ o ʒɑ̃bɔ̃.
Black. And a ham sandwich.

14. — Et un paquet de cigarettes, s.v.p.
e œ̃ pakɛ t sigarɛt, . . .
And a package of cigarettes, please.

lit est confortable, *this bed is comfortable.* [5] **café crème = café au lait** [o lɛ]. [6] **sandwich au fromage** [frɔmaːʒ], *cheese sandwich;* **de la pâtisserie** [pɑtisri], *pastry, cakes;* **une pâtisserie,** *pastry shop; tearoom;* **petits fours** [pti fuːr], *small cakes, fancy cakes.*

LE PETIT DÉJEUNER

Breakfast

1. — A quelle heure le petit déjeuner?
   a kɛl œːr lə pti deʒœne?
   What time is breakfast?
2. — Quand vous voudrez,[1] monsieur.
   kɑ̃ vu vudre, məsjø.
   Any time you wish, sir.
3. — Puis-je [2] être servi maintenant?
   pɥi ʒ ɛt(r) sɛrvi mɛ̃tnɑ̃?
   May I be served now?
4. — Certainement. Dans la salle à manger?
   sɛrtɛnmɑ̃. dɑ̃ la sal a mɑ̃ʒe?
   Certainly. In the dining room?
5. — Non, dans ma chambre.
   nɔ̃, dɑ̃ ma ʃɑ̃ːbr.
   No, in my room.
6. — Du café au lait ou du chocolat?
   dy kafe o lɛ u dy ʃɔkɔla?
   Coffee (with hot milk) or chocolate?
7. — Je prendrai [3] du café au lait.
   ʒ(ə) prɑ̃dre dy kafe o lɛ.
   I'll take coffee.

[1] § 26*d*. [2] From **pouvoir,** § 40. [3] Future of **prendre,** § 35, III. [4] Partitive, § 2*i*; **un œuf** [œ̃n‿œf], *an egg;* **des œufs à la coque** [dez‿ø a la kɔk], *boiled eggs,* **brouillés** [bruje], *scrambled,* **sur le plat** [syr lə pla], *fried.* [5] **pamplemousse** [pɑ̃pləmus], *f. grapefruit;* **con-**

8. — Bien, monsieur. Et ensuite?
bjɛ̃, məsjø. e ɑ̃sɥit?
Very well, sir. And what else (lit. 'next')?

9. — Pouvez-vous me servir des œufs? [4]
puve vu m(ə) sɛrviːr dez‿ø?
Can you serve me eggs?

10. — Ah, non, monsieur, pas le matin.
ɑ, nɔ̃, məsjø, pɑ l(ə) matɛ̃.
Oh no, sir, not in the morning.

11. — Vous avez du jus d'orange? [5]
vuz‿ave dy ʒy d ɔrɑ̃ːʒ?
Have you any orange juice?

12. — Non, monsieur; je regrette.
nɔ̃, məsjø; ʒə r(ə)grɛt.
No, sir, I'm sorry.

13. — Vous avez du pain grillé?
vuz‿ave dy pɛ̃ grije?
Have you any toast?

14. — Seulement des croissants et du beurre.
sœlmɑ̃ de krwasɑ̃ e dy bœːr.
Only (crescent-shaped) rolls and butter.

fiture, *f. preserve(s), jam.* For other articles of food, see Appendix, § 41. The typical French breakfast consists of **café au lait** or **chocolat,** and **croissants** (*crescent-shaped rolls*) or buttered bread.

LE DÎNER (*a*)

Dinner (*a*)

1. — Ce restaurant est très chic.
sə rɛstɔrɑ̃ ɛ trɛ ʃik.
This restaurant is very elegant.
2. — Voici le maître d'hôtel.
vwasi l(ə) mɛt(r) d otɛl.
Here's the head waiter.
3. — Une table pour deux, s.v.p.
yn tabl pur dø, . . .
A table for two, please.
4. — (*Le maître d'hôtel*) Par ici, messieurs.
(lə mɛtr d otɛl) par isi, mesjø.
(The head waiter) *This way, gentlemen.*
5. — Nous serons très bien ici.
nu s(ə)rɔ̃ trɛ bjɛ̃ isi.
We'll be very comfortable here.
6. — Garçon, la carte du jour, s.v.p.
garsɔ̃ la kart dy ʒuːr, . . .
Waiter, the menu, please.
7. — (*Le garçon*) Ces messieurs ont choisi?
(lə garsɔ̃) se mesjø ɔ̃ ʃwazi?
(The waiter) *Have you gentlemen selected?*

[1] For a list of other foods and drinks, see § 41. [2] **vin blanc** [blɑ̃] (**rosé** [rozé], **sec** [sɛk], **doux** [du]), *white* (*rose, dry, sweet*) *wine.*

Additional words: **un couvert = une serviette** [sɛrvjɛt], *napkin;*

8\. — Moi, je prends des huîtres.[1]
mwa, ʒ(ə) prɑ̃ dez‿ɥiːtr.
I'll take oysters.

9\. — Un potage pour moi.
œ̃ pɔtaːʒ pur mwa.
Soup for me.

10\. — (*Le garçon*) Et comme plat de viande?
(lə garsɔ̃) e kɔm pla d(ə) vjɑ̃ːd?
(The waiter) *And for your meat dish?*

11\. — Nous n'avons pas encore choisi.
nu n avɔ̃ pɑ(z) ɑ̃kɔːr ʃwazi.
We haven't selected (it) yet.

12\. — Bien, messieurs. Et comme boisson?
bjɛ̃, mesjø. e kɔm bwasɔ̃?
Very well, (gentlemen). And your drink?

13\. — Un demi-litre de rouge [2] pour moi.
œ̃ dmi lit(r) də ruːʒ pur mwa.
Half a bottle of red wine for me.

14\. — Je ne bois pas de vin. De la bière.
ʒə n(ə) bwa pɑ d vɛ̃. d(ə) la bjɛːr.
I don't drink wine. Beer.

un couteau [kuto], *knife;* **une fourchette** [furʃɛt], *fork;* **une grande cuillère** [grɑ̃ːd kɥijɛːr], *soupspoon;* **une petite cuillère** [ptit kɥijɛːr], *teaspoon;* **un verre** [vɛːr], *glass;* **une assiette** [asjɛt], *plate.*

LE DÎNER (*b*)

Dinner (*b*)

1\. — (*Le garçon*) Vous avez choisi, messieurs?
(lə garsɔ̃) vuz‿ ave ʃwazi, mesjø?
(The waiter) *Have you made your selection?*

2\. — Un gigot de mouton.
œ̃ ʒigo d(ə) mutɔ̃.
Leg of lamb.

3\. — Je ne mange pas de viande.
ʒə n(ə) mɑ̃ːʒ pɑ d vjɑ̃ːd.
I don't eat meat.

4\. — (*Le garçon*) Le poisson est très frais.
(lə garsɔ̃) lə pwasɔ̃ ɛ trɛ frɛ.
(The waiter) *The fish is very fresh.*

5\. — Apportez-moi une truite meunière.
apɔrte mwa yn trɥit mønjɛːr.
Bring me trout meunière.

6\. — (*Le garçon*) Et comme légumes?
(lə garsɔ̃) e kɔm legym?
(The waiter) *And your vegetables?*

7\. — Des haricots verts pour moi.
de ariko vɛːr pur mwa.
String beans for me.

8\. — Des pommes (de terre) à l'anglaise.
de pɔm (də tɛːr) a l ɑ̃glɛːz.
Boiled potatoes (lit. 'potatoes in the English style').

9\. — (*Le garçon*) Et ensuite, messieurs?
(lə garsɔ̃) e ɑ̃sɥit, mesjø?
(The waiter) *And after that?*

10\. — Une salade de laitue. Et un camembert.
yn salad d(ə) lɛty. e œ̃ kamɑ̃bɛːr.
Lettuce salad. And Camembert cheese.

11\. — Pour moi aussi. Mais pas de fromage.
pur mwa osi. mɛ pɑ d frɔmaːʒ.
The same for me. But no cheese.

12\. — (*Le garçon*) Et comme dessert?
(lə garsɔ̃) e kɔm desɛːr?
(The waiter) *And your dessert?*

13\. — Des fraises à la crème.
de frɛːz a la krɛm.
Strawberries and cream.

14\. — Et moi, une glace à la vanille.
e mwa, yn glas a la vaniːj.
And I'll take vanilla ice cream.

15\. — Garçon, l'addition, s.v.p.!
garsɔ̃, l adisjɔ̃, . . .
Waiter, the check, please!

16\. — Voilà, messieurs.
vwala, mesjø.
There you are, gentlemen.

A LA BANQUE (*a*)

At the Bank (a)

1. — J'ai ici une lettre de crédit.
   ʒ e isi yn lɛt(r) də kredi.
   I have a letter of credit here.
2. — Combien voulez-vous retirer?
   kɔ̃bjɛ̃ vule vu rətire?
   How much do you wish to withdraw?
3. — Quel est le taux du change?
   kɛl ɛ l(ə) to dy ʃɑ̃ːʒ?
   What is the rate of exchange?
4. — Trente francs quinze le dollar.
   trɑ̃ːt frɑ̃ kɛ̃ːz lə dɔlaːr.
   Thirty francs fifteen (centimes) to the dollar.
5. — Le franc a monté, n'est-ce pas?
   lə frɑ̃ a mɔ̃te, n ɛ s pɑ?
   The franc has risen, hasn't it?
6. — Il peut baisser brusquement.
   i(l) pø bɛse bryskəmɑ̃.
   It may fall suddenly.
7. — Cent dollars, ça fait combien de francs?
   sɑ̃ dɔlaːr, sa fɛ kɔ̃bjɛ̃ d(ə) frɑ̃?
   A hundred dollars, that makes how many francs?
8. — Trois mille quinze francs.
   trwɑ mil kɛ̃ːz frɑ̃.
   Three thousand and fifteen francs.

9. — Je voudrais aussi toucher un chèque.
ʒ(ə) vudrɛ osi tuʃe œ̃ ʃɛk.
I should also like to cash a check.

10. — Voulez-vous l'endosser, je vous prie.
vule vu l ɑ̃dɔse, ʒ(ə) vu pri.
Will you endorse it, please.

11. — Voilà.
vwala.
There you are.

12. — Voici votre numéro. Prenez-le.
vwasi vɔt(r) nymero. prəne lə.
Here's your number. Take it.

13. — Qu'est-ce que je dois en faire?
k ɛ s kə ʒ(ə) dwaz‿ɑ̃ fɛːr?
What must I do with it?

14. — Présentez-le au guichet des payements.
prezɑ̃te lə o giʃɛ de pɛjmɑ̃.
Present it at the window marked "Payments."

15. — (*L'employé au guichet*) Dix-huit!
(l ɑ̃plwaje o giʃɛ) dizɥit!
(The clerk at the window) *Eighteen!*

16. — C'est moi le dix-huit.
s ɛ mwa l(ə) diz ɥit.
I'm (number) eighteen.

A LA BANQUE (*b*)

At the Bank (b)

1. — Je voudrais ouvrir un compte.
   ʒ(ə) vudrɛ(z) uvriːr œ̃ kɔ̃ːt.
   I'd like to open an account.
2. — Bien. Nous payons deux pour cent.
   bjɛ̃. nu pɛjɔ̃ dø pur sɑ̃.
   Very well. We pay two per cent.
3. — Ce n'est pas très avantageux.
   sə n ɛ pɑ trɛz‿avɑ̃taʒø.
   That's not very profitable.
4. — Ah, mais, c'est de toute sécurité.
   ɑ, mɛ, s ɛ də tut sekyrite.
   Oh, but it's very safe.
5. — Je voudrais déposer mille dollars.
   ʒ(ə) vudrɛ depoze mil dɔlaːr.
   I'd like to deposit a thousand dollars.
6. — Je vous donnerai un livret de banque.
   ʒ(ə) vu dɔnre œ̃ livrɛ d(ə) bɑ̃ːk.
   I'll give you a passbook
7. — Et un carnet de chèques, s.v.p.
   e œ̃ karnɛ d(ə) ʃɛk, ...
   And a checkbook, please.

Additional words: **l'action,** *f. share;* **le banquier** [bɑ̃kje], *banker;* **le billet** [bijɛ] **de banque,** *bank note;* **la bourse** [burs], *(stock) exchange;* **le changeur** [ʃɑ̃ʒœːr], *money changer;* **l'emprunt** [ɑ̃prœ̃], *m. loan;* **emprunter** [ɑ̃prœ̃te], *to loan;* **les frais** [frɛ], *m. pl. expenses,*

8. — Certainement. En voici un.
sɛrtɛnmɑ̃. ɑ̃ vwasi œ̃.
Certainly. Here's one.

9. — Cette banque a des succursales?
sɛt bɑ̃ːk a de sykyrsal?
Has this bank any branches?

10. — Dans toutes les grandes villes.
dɑ̃ tut le grɑ̃ːd vil.
In all the large cities.

11. — C'est bien commode quand on voyage.
s ɛ bjɛ̃ kɔmɔd kɑ̃t‿ ɔ̃ vwajaːʒ.
That's very convenient when a person travels.

12. — Surtout pour toucher vos chèques.
syrtu pur tuʃe vo ʃɛk.
Especially for cashing your checks.

13. — Alors, je n'aurai pas de difficultés?
alɔːr, ʒ(ə) n ɔre pɑ d difikylte?
Then I'll have no trouble?

14. — Pas du tout, je vous assure.
pɑ dy tu, ʒ(ə) vuz‿ asyːr.
None at all, I assure you.

le mont-de-piété [mɔ̃d(ə)pjete], *pawnshop;* **l'obligation** [ɔbligɑsjɔ̃], *f. bond;* **prêter** [prɛte], *to lend;* **pouvez-vous me prêter?** [puve vu m(ə) prɛte], *can you lend me?* **la rente** [rɑ̃ːt], *income;* **la taxe, l'impôt** *m.* [taks, ɛ̃po], *tax.*

CHEZ LE COIFFEUR

In the Barbershop

1. — Faut-il attendre longtemps?
   fot‿ i(l) atɑ̃ːdr lɔ̃tɑ̃?
   Must I wait long?
2. — C'est votre tour, monsieur.
   s ɛ vɔt(r) tuːr, məsjø.
   It's your turn, sir.
3. — Une taille de cheveux, s.v.p.
   yn tɑːj də ʃvø, ...
   A haircut, please.
4. — Comment faut-il les tailler?[1]
   kɔmɑ̃ fot‿ i(l) le tɑje?
   How should it be cut?
5. — Court par derrière, long par devant.
   kuːr par dɛrjɛːr, lɔ̃ par d(ə)vɑ̃.
   Short in back, long in front.
6. — Je passe[2] la tondeuse sur la nuque?
   ʒ(ə) pɑːs la tɔ̃døːz syr la nyk?
   Shall I use the clippers on the back (of the neck)?
7. — Oui, mais pas sur les côtés.
   wi, mɛ pɑ syr le kote.
   Yes, but not on the sides.

[1] **tailler,** *to cut, trim* = **couper** [kupe], *to cut, cut off.* [2] Interrogation, § 23*b*.

Additional words: **un rasoir mécanique** [razwaːr mekanik], *safety*

8. — Est-ce assez comme cela?
ɛ s ase kɔm sla?
Is that enough?

9. — Taillez encore un peu sur le devant.
taje ɑ̃kɔːr œ̃ pø syr lə d(ə)vɑ̃.
Cut off a little more in front.

10. — Une friction? Un shampooing?
yn friksjɔ̃? œ̃ ʃɑ̃pwɛ̃?
A rub (massage)? A shampoo?

11. — Merci. Laissez les cheveux à sec.
mɛrsi. lɛse le ʃvø a sɛk.
No, thank you. Leave it dry.

12. — La raie à droite, à gauche, au milieu?
la rɛ a drwɑt, a goːʃ, o miljø?
The part on the right, left, or in the middle?

13. — Peignez tout droit en arrière.
pɛɲe tu drwɑ ɑ̃n‿arjɛːr.
Comb it straight back.

14. — Bon. Voilà qui est fait.
bɔ̃. vwala ki ɛ fɛ.
There. All ready.

razor; **un rasoir électrique** [elɛktrik], *electric razor;* **un pourboire** [purbwaːr], *tip;* **la lotion** [lɔsjɔ̃], *lotion;* **friser** [frize], *to curl;* **savonner** [savɔne], *to soap, lather;* **le savon à barbe,** *shaving soap.*

LE SALON DE BEAUTÉ (*a*)

The Beauty Parlor (a)

1. — Puis-je avoir une permanente?
pɥi ʒ avwaːr yn pɛrmanɑ̃ːt?
May I have a permanent?
2. — Passez dans ce cabinet, je vous prie.
pɑse dɑ̃ s(ə) kabinɛ, ʒ(ə) vu pri.
Come into this booth, please.
3. — Mes cheveux sont horribles.
me ʃvø sɔ̃t‿ ɔribl.
My hair is terrible.
4. — Oh, non, madame, mais un peu huileux.
o, nɔ̃, madam, mɛ(z)‿œ̃ pø ɥilø.
Oh, no, madam, but it's a little oily.
5. — Il faudrait un bon shampooing?
i(l) fodrɛ œ̃ bɔ̃ ʃɑ̃pwɛ̃?
Does it need a good shampoo?
6. — Ah, oui! Quelle coiffure désirez-vous?
ɑ wi! kɛl kwafyːr dezire vu?
Oh, yes! What style coiffure do you prefer?
7. — Lissez-moi les cheveux en arrière.
lise mwa le ʃvø ɑ̃n‿arjɛːr.
Smooth the hair straight back.
8. — Je vais les friser [1] sur le front?
ʒ(ə) vɛ le frize syr lə frɔ̃?
Shall I curl it on the forehead?

9. — Non. Sur les tempes et la nuque.
nɔ̃. syr le tɑ̃ːp e la nyk.
No. Over the temples and in the back (of the neck).

10. — Cette coiffure vous va très bien.
sɛt kwafyːr vu va trɛ bjɛ̃.
This style is very becoming to you.

11. — Vous trouvez? Ça fait assez jeune?
vu truve? sa fɛ ase ʒœn?
You think so? Does it make me look younger?

12. — Ça fait très jeune fille.
sa fɛ trɛ ʒœn fiːj.
It makes you look like a young girl.

13. — Donnez-moi un facial aussi.
dɔne mwa œ̃ fasjal osi.
Give me a facial too.

14. — Bien, madame. Comme vous voudrez.
bjɛ̃, madam. kɔm vu vudre.
Very well, madam. As you wish.

15. — Attention! Vous me brûlez!
atɑ̃sjɔ̃! vu m(ə) bryle!
Be careful! You're burning me!

16. — Oh, pardon! L'eau est très chaude.
o, pardɔ̃! l o ɛ trɛ ʃoːd.
Oh, pardon me. The water is very hot.

LE SALON DE BEAUTÉ (*b*)

The Beauty Parlor (b)

1. — Vous avez la peau très douce, madame.
   vuz‿ ave la po trɛ dus, madam.
   Your skin is very tender, madam.
2. — Mais j'ai des rides affreuses!
   mɛ ʒe de riːd afrøːz!
   But I have awful wrinkles!
3. — Nous allons enlever ça.
   nuz‿ alɔ̃(z) ɑ̃lve sa.
   We'll get rid of them.
4. — Quelle crème recommandez-vous?
   kɛl krɛm rəkɔmɑ̃de vu?
   What cream do you recommend?
5. — Celle-ci. Elle est merveilleuse.
   sɛl si. ɛl ɛ mɛrvɛjøːz.
   This one. It is wonderful.
6. — Voulez-vous appeler la manucure?
   vule vu(z) aple la manykyːr?
   Will you call the manicurist?
7. — Oui, madame, tout de suite.
   wi, madam, tu t sɥit.
   Yes, madam, right away.

[1] **je vous fais les ongles** [ʒ(ə) vu fɛ lez‿ɔ̃ːgl]? = **voulez-vous que je vous fasse** [fas] **les ongles?** *shall I do your nails?* § 27*a*; **se faire les ongles,** *to trim one's nails.* [2] **noir, –e** [nwaːr], *black;* **bleu, –e**

8. — (*La manucure*) Les ongles,[1] madame?
(la manykyːr) lez‿ɔ̃ːgl, madam?
(The manicurist) *Your nails, madam?*

9. — Oui, pendant que mes cheveux sèchent.
wi, pɑ̃dɑ̃ k(ə) me ʃvø sɛːʃ.
Yes, while my hair is drying.

10. — Quelle couleur désirez-vous?
kɛl kulœːr dezire vu?
What color do you wish?

11. — Je ne sais pas. Rose, rouge?[2]
ʒə n se pɑ. roːz, ruːʒ?
I don't know. Rose, red?

12. — Le rose vous va très bien, madame.
lə roːz vu va trɛ bjɛ̃, madam.
Rose is very becoming to you, madam.

13. — Le rose va avec mon teint?
lə roːz va avɛk mɔ̃ tɛ̃?
Does rose go with my complexion?

14. — Oui, madame, et c'est très distingué.
wi, madam, e s ɛ trɛ distɛ̃ge.
Yes, madam, and it's very distinguished.

[blø], *blue;* **blanc, blanche** [blɑ̃, blɑ̃ːʃ], *white;* **vert, verte** [vɛːr, vɛrt], *green;* **jaune** [ʒoːn], *yellow;* **brun, brune** [brœ̃, bryn], *brown;* **gris, grise** [gri, griːz], *gray.*

LA VISITE

The Visit

1. — Monsieur Machin est-il chez lui?
məsjø maʃɛ̃ ɛt‿i(l) ʃe lɥi?
Is Mr. So-and-So at home?
2. — Oui, monsieur. Entrez, je vous prie.
wi, məsjø. ɑ̃tre, ʒ(ə) vu pri.
Yes, sir. Come in, please.
3. — (*Monsieur Machin*) Bonjour, monsieur.
(məsjø maʃɛ̃) bɔ̃ʒuːr, məsjø.
(Mr. So-and-So) *How do you do, sir.*
4. — Permettez-moi . . .
pɛrmɛte mwa . . .
Allow me . . .
5. — Ah! une lettre de mon ami!
ɑ! yn lɛtr(ə) d(ə) mɔ̃n‿ami!
Oh! a letter from my friend!
6. — Il vous présente ses amitiés.
i(l) vu prezɑ̃ːt sez‿amitje.
He sends you his best wishes.
7. — Asseyez-vous donc. Comment va-t-il?
asɛje vu dɔ̃ːk. kɔmɑ̃ va t i(l)?
Do sit down. How is he?
8. — Très bien. C'est un de mes bons amis.
trɛ bjɛ̃. sɛt‿ œ̃ d(ə) me bɔ̃z‿ ami.
Very well. He's one of my good friends.

9. — Vous êtes le bienvenu chez moi.
vuz‿ ɛt lə bjɛ̃vny ʃe mwa.
Welcome to my home.

10. — J'espère que je ne vous dérange pas.
ʒ ɛspɛːr k(ə) ʒə n vu derɑ̃ːʒ pɑ.
I hope I'm not troubling you.

11. — Pas du tout. Pouvez-vous rester dîner?
pɑ dy tu. puve vu rɛste dine?
Not at all. Can you stay for dinner?

12. — Merci. Je ne suis pas libre ce soir.
mɛrsi. ʒə n sɥi pɑ liːbr sə swaːr.
No, thank you. I'm not free this evening.

13. — Eh bien, à une autre fois alors.
e bjɛ̃, a yn ot(r) fwa alɔːr.
Well, some other time then.

14. — Vous êtes trop aimable.
vuz‿ ɛt trop‿ɛmabl.
You are very kind.

15. — Alors, à bientôt.
alɔːr, a bjɛ̃to.
I hope to see you soon.

16. — C'est ça. Au revoir.
s ɛ sa. o r(ə)vwaːr.
Very well. Good-bye.

LA BLANCHISSEUSE

The Laundress

1. — C'est vous la blanchisseuse?
   s ɛ vu la blɑ̃ʃisøːz?
   Are you the laundress?
2. — Oui, monsieur. Vous avez du linge sale?
   wi, məsjø. vuz‿ ave dy lɛ̃ːʒ sal?
   Yes, sir. Have you any dirty clothes?
3. — Oui, tout est dans ce paquet.
   wi, tut‿ ɛ dɑ̃ s(ə) pakɛ.
   Yes, it's all in this bundle.
4. — Vous avez fait une liste?
   vuz‿ ave fɛ(t) yn list?
   Have you made out a list?
5. — Oui, la voilà.
   wi, la vwala.
   Yes, here it is.
6. — Vous n'êtes pas trop pressé?
   vu n ɛt pɑ tro prese?
   You're not in too much of a hurry?
7. — Ah si, je n'ai plus de linge propre.
   ɑ si, ʒ(ə) n e ply d lɛ̃ːʒ prɔpr.
   Yes, I am; I have no more clean linen.

Additional words: **le bas** [bɑ], *stocking;* **la blouse** [bluːz], *waist, blouse;* **les calçons** [kalsɔ̃], *shorts;* **coudre** [kuːdr], *to sew;* **donner un coup de fer** [dɔne œ̃ ku d(ə) fɛːr], *to press;* **enlever les taches (d'encre)** [ɑ̃lve le taʃ (dɑ̃ːkr)], *to remove the (ink) spots;* **le fer à repasser** [rəpɑse], *flatiron;* **la planche** [plɑ̃ːʃ] **à repasser,** *ironing*

8. — Alors, vous l'aurez après demain.
alɔːr, vu l ɔre aprɛ dmɛ̃.
In that case, you'll have it the day after tomorrow.

9. — Faites attention aux chaussettes.
fɛt(s) atɑ̃sjɔ̃ o ʃosɛt.
Be careful of the socks.

10. — Je lave toute la soie à l'eau tiède.
ʒ(ə) laːv tut la swa a l o tjɛːd.
I wash all silk in lukewarm water.

11. — Et pas d'amidon sur les chemises.
e pɑ d amidɔ̃ syr le ʃmiːz.
And no starch in the shirts.

12. — Comment voulez-vous les cols?
kɔmɑ̃ vule vu le kɔl?
How do you want the collars?

13. — Repassez-les sans amidon.
rəpɑse le sɑ̃z‿amidɔ̃.
Iron them without starch.

14. — Bien, monsieur. Au revoir, monsieur.
bjɛ̃, məsjø. o r(ə)vwaːr, məsjø.
Very well, sir. Good-bye, (sir).

board; **le mouchoir** [muʃwaːr], *handkerchief;* **la jupe** [ʒyp], *skirt;* **le pyjama** [piʒama], *pajamas;* **raccommoder** [rakɔmɔde], *to mend, darn;* **stopper** [stɔpe], *to repair by invisible mending;* **le stoppage** [stɔpaːʒ], *invisible mending.*

LA VISITE AU MUSÉE [1]

The Visit to the Museum

1. — L'entrée du musée est-elle [2] gratuite?
l ɑ̃tre dy myze ɛt‿ɛl gratɥit?
Is admission to the museum free?
2. — Les dimanches et jours de fête.
le dimɑ̃ːʃ e ʒuːr də fɛt.
Sundays and holidays.
3. — Les autres jours, combien paye-t-on?
lez ot(r) ʒuːr, kɔ̃bjɛ̃ pɛj t ɔ̃?
What's the admission the other days?
4. — Les jours de semaine, dix francs.
le ʒuːr də smɛːn, di frɑ̃.
On weekdays, ten francs.
5. — Quelles sont les heures de visite?
kɛl sɔ̃ lez‿œːr d(ə) vizit?
What are the visiting hours?
6. — De dix heures à midi et de deux à cinq.
də diz‿œːr a midi e də dø a sɛ̃ːk.
From ten to twelve and from two to five.
7. — Où peut-on acheter un catalogue?
u pøt‿ɔ̃ aʃte œ̃ katalɔg?
Where can I buy a catalogue?

[1] The chief art museums in Paris are: **Le musée du Louvre** [luːvr]; **le musée du Luxembourg** [lyksɑ̃buːr]; **le musée de Cluny** [klyni]. [2] § 23*c*. [3] **le peintre** [pɛ̃ːtr], *painter;* **le tableau** [tablo], *picture;* **le paysage** [peizaːʒ], *landscape;* **la peinture à l'huile** [a

8. — Ici. En voici un.
isi. ɑ̃ vwasi œ̃.
Here. Here's one.

9. — Où sont les peintures [3] modernes?
u sɔ̃ le pɛ̃tyːr mɔdɛrn?
Where are the modern paintings?

10. — Galerie F. Demandez au gardien.
galri ɛf. d(ə)mɑ̃de(z) o gardjɛ̃.
Gallery F. Ask the custodian.

11. — Et où se trouvent les sculptures?
e u s(ə) truːv le skyltyːr?
And where is the sculpture?

12. — Dans l'aile nord. Prenez un guide.
dɑ̃ l ɛːl nɔːr. prəne(z) œ̃ gid.
In the north wing. Take a guide.

13. — Faut-il lui donner un pourboire?
fot‿ i(l) lɥi dɔne œ̃ purbwaːr?
Must one give him a tip?

14. — Naturellement.
natyrɛlmɑ̃.
Of course.

lɥil], *oil painting;* **une aquarelle** [akwarɛl], *water color;* **une nature morte** [natyːr mɔrt], *still life;* **le cadre** [kɑːdr], *frame;* **étudier la peinture,** *to study painting;* **faire de la peinture,** *to paint.*

AU BUREAU DE TÉLÉGRAPHE

At the Telegraph Office

1. — Je voudrais envoyer un télégramme.[1]
ʒ(ə) vudrɛ(z) ɑ̃vwaje œ̃ telegram.
I should like to send a telegram.

2. — Bien. Écrivez-le sur ce formulaire.
bjɛ̃. ekrive lə syr sə fɔrmylɛːr.
Very well. Write it out on this blank.

3. — Combien pour une dépêche [1] de jour?
kɔ̃bjɛ̃ pur yn depɛʃ də ʒuːr?
How much is a day message?

4. — Trente francs les dix mots.
trɑ̃ːt frɑ̃ le di mo.
Thirty francs for ten words.

5. — Et une dépêche de nuit?
e yn depɛʃ də nɥi?
And a night letter?

6. — Ah oui, ça coûte moitié moins cher.
ɑ wi, sa kut mwatje mwɛ̃ ʃɛːr.
Oh, yes, that costs half as much.

7. — Est-ce qu'on peut câbler à New York?
ɛ s k ɔ̃ pø kɑble a nœ jɔrk?
Can one cable to New York?

[1] **un télégramme = une dépêche; un radiogramme** [radjɔgram], *wireless message;* **un message chiffré** [mɛsaːʒ ʃifre], *ciphered* or *code message;* **télégraphier** [telegrafje], *to wire, cable;* **le télégraphiste** [telegrafist], *telegraph operator;* **le facteur** [faktœːr] **télégraphiste,**

8. — Certainement, à vingt francs le mot.
sɛrtɛnmɑ̃, a vɛ̃ frɑ̃ l(ə) mo.
Certainly, twenty francs a word.

9. — Et pour un câblegramme différé?
e pur œ̃ kɑbləgram difere?
And for a deferred cablegram?

10. — Un différé est moitié prix.
œ̃ difere ɛ mwatje pri.
A deferred is half price.

11. — Avec réponse payée, c'est combien?
avɛk repɔ̃ːs pɛjɛ, s ɛ kɔ̃bjɛ̃?
How much is it with the reply prepaid?

12. — Eh bien, ça coûte le double.
e bjɛ̃, sa kut lə dubl.
Well, that costs twice as much.

13. — A quelle heure se ferme le bureau?
a kɛl œːr sə fɛrm lə byro?
What time does the office close?

14. — Ce bureau est ouvert jour et nuit.
sə byro ɛt‿uvɛːr ʒuːr e nɥi.
This office is open day and night.

telegraph messenger; **télégraphie sans fil** [sɑ̃ fil] = **T.S.F.**, *wireless telegraphy, radio;* **le sans-fil**, *wireless message;* **rédiger** [rediʒe], *to write, compose;* **le tarif** [tarif] **télégraphique**, *telegraph rates.*

LE CINÉMA

The Movies

1. — Voulez-vous aller au cinéma [1] ce soir?
vule vu(z) ale o sinema sə swaːr?
Do you want to go to the movies this evening?

2. — Je veux bien. Quel film donne-t-on?
ʒ(ə) vø bjɛ̃. kɛl film dɔn t ɔ̃?
I'd like to. What picture are they giving?

3. — Avez-vous vu «La Femme fantôme»?
ave vu vy la fam fɑ̃toːm?
Have you seen "The Phantom Woman"?

4. — Non. Est-ce un drame ou une comédie?
nɔ̃. ɛ s œ̃ dram u yn kɔmedi?
No. Is it a drama or a comedy?

5. — C'est un drame historique, je crois.
s ɛt‿œ̃ dram istɔrik, ʒə krwɑ.
It's a historical drama, I believe.

6. — Quelles sont les vedettes qui y jouent?
kɛl sɔ̃ le vədɛt ki i ʒu?
Who are the stars that play in it?

7. — L'héroïne est Georgette Solage.
l erɔin ɛ ʒɔrʒɛt sɔlaːʒ.
The heroine is Georgette Solage.

[1] **le guichet** [giʃɛ], *ticket window;* **une ouvreuse** [uvrøːz], *usher* (woman); **film d'actualités** [film daktɥalite], *newsreel;* **dessins animés** [desɛ̃ anime], *cartoon;* **ennuyeux, –euse** [ɑ̃nɥijø, –øːz], *boring, dull;* **un entr'acte** [ɑ̃trakt], *intermission;* **épatant** [epatɑ̃],

8. — Ah, c'est mon actrice favorite!
ɑ, s ɛ mɔ̃n‿aktris favɔrit!
Oh, she's my favorite actress!

9. — Et Paul Morin joue le rôle du héros.
e pɔl mɔrɛ̃ ʒu l(ə) roːl dy ero.
And Paul Morin plays the role of the hero.

10. — C'est un acteur de premier ordre.
s ɛt‿œ̃n‿aktœːr də prəmjɛːr‿ɔrdr.
He's a first-class actor.

11. — Ça commence à huit heures.
sa kɔmɑ̃ːs a ɥit‿œːr.
It begins at eight o'clock.

12. — Vous avez les billets d'entrée?
vuz‿ave le bijɛ d ɑ̃tre?
Have you the tickets?

13. — Non. On va faire la queue.
nɔ̃. ɔ̃ va fɛːr la kø.
No. We'll stand in line.

14. — Bien. Passez chez moi à sept heures.
bjɛ̃. pɑse ʃe mwa a sɛt œːr.
All right. Call for me at seven o'clock.

wonderful, splendid; **ce n'est pas bien épatant,** *it's nothing to write home about;* **le rang** [rɑ̃], *row;* **voilà qu'on sonne** [sɔn], *the bell is ringing;* **saisissant, –ante** [sɛzisɑ̃, –ɑ̃ːt], *gripping, thrilling.*

LE KIOSQUE A JOURNAUX [1]

The Newsstand

1. — Je voudrais acheter un journal.
ʒ(ə) vudrɛ(z) aʃte œ̃ ʒurnal.
I'd like to buy a newspaper.
2. — Voilà justement un kiosque.
vwala ʒystəmɑ̃ œ̃ kjɔsk.
There's a paper stand right there.
3. — (*A la marchande*) Le « New York Herald » ?
(a la marʃɑ̃ːd) lə nœ jɔrk erald?
(To the vendor) *The "New York Herald"?*
4. — Ah, monsieur, il n'en reste plus.
ɑ, məsjø, i(l) n ɑ̃ rɛst ply.
I haven't any left, sir.
5. — Quel journal du matin vous reste-t-il ?
kɛl ʒurnal dy matɛ̃ vu rɛst t i(l)?
What morning paper have you left?
6. — « Le Temps », « Le Figaro », « L'Humanité ».
lə tɑ̃, lə figaro, l ymanite.
"Le Temps," "Le Figaro," "L'Humanité."
7. — « Le Figaro ». Voici cinq francs.
lə figaro. vwasi sɛ̃ frɑ̃.
"Le Figaro." Here are five francs.

[1] **un abonnement** [abɔnmɑ̃], *subscription;* **un abonné** [abɔne], *subscriber, holder of a season ticket;* **la manchette** [mɑ̃ʃɛt], *headline;* **une revue** [rəvy], *magazine;* **une annonce** [anɔ̃ːs], *advertisement;* **annoncer** [anɔ̃se], *to advertise;* **interviewer** [ɛ̃tɛrvjue], *to interview;*

8. — **Voilà votre monnaie.**
vwala vɔt(r) mɔnɛ.
Here's your change.

9. — **Merci, madame. Voyons les nouvelles.**
mɛrsi, madam. vwajɔ̃ le nuvɛl.
Thank you, (madam). Let's look at the news.

10. — **La politique ne m'intéresse pas.**
la pɔlitik nə m ɛ̃terɛs pɑ.
Politics do not interest me.

11. — **Vous préférez les courses de chevaux.**
vu prefere le kurs də ʃvo.
You prefer horse races.

12. — **Demain c'est la course de Longchamp.**
d(ə)mɛ̃ s ɛ la kurs də lɔ̃ʃɑ̃.
Tomorrow is the Longchamp race.

13. — **Le journal ne parle que de ça.**
lə ʒurnal nə parl kə d(ə) sa.
The paper speaks of nothing but that.

14. — **Il faut y aller. Le tout Paris y va.**
i(l) fot‿i ale. lə tu pari i va.
We'll have to go. All Paris is going.

on demande [ɔ̃ d(ə)mɑ̃ːd], *wanted;* **à vendre** [a vɑ̃ːdr], *for sale;* **à louer** [a lue, lwe], *for rent;* **loué** [lue, lwe], *engaged, reserved;* **réclame** [reklɑːm], *advertisement;* **faire de la réclame,** *to advertise, boost.*

CHEZ LE LIBRAIRE [1]

At the Bookseller's

1. — Est-ce qu'on peut examiner ce livre?
ɛ s k ɔ̃ pø(t) egzamine sə liːvr?
May I look at this book?

2. — Mais oui, monsieur, faites donc.
mɛ wi, məsjø, fɛt dɔ̃ːk.
Yes, sir, go right ahead.

3. — C'est une ancienne édition?
s ɛt‿yn ɑ̃sjɛn edisjɔ̃?
Is it an old edition?

4. — Une première édition, très rare.
yn prəmjɛːr edisjɔ̃, trɛ rɑːr.
A first edition, very rare.

5. — La reliure [2] est un peu endommagée.
la rəljyːr ɛt‿œ̃ pø ɑ̃dɔmaʒe.
The binding is a little damaged.

6. — Ce n'est rien. Ça peut se réparer.
sə n ɛ rjɛ̃. sa pø s(ə) repare.
That's nothing. That can be repaired.

7. — Vous avez aussi des ouvrages modernes?
vuz‿ ave(z) osi dez‿uvraːʒ mɔdɛrn?
Have you also modern works?

[1] **le bouquiniste** [bukinist], *second-hand bookdealer;* **livre d'occasion** [dɔkɑzjɔ̃], *second-hand book.* [2] **livre broché** [brɔʃe], *paper-bound book;* **la brochure** [brɔʃyːr], *pamphlet;* **relier** [rəlje], *to bind;* **relié en veau** [rəlje ɑ̃ vo], *bound in calf;* **en toile** [ɑ̃ twal], *in cloth;*

8. — Certainement; roman, poésie, théâtre[3] . . .
sɛrtɛnmɑ̃; rɔmɑ̃, pɔezi, teɑːtr . . .
Certainly; novels, poetry, plays . . .

9. — Avez-vous les œuvres de Balzac?
ave vu lez‿œːvr də balzak?
Have you the works of Balzac?

10. — Voici une édition en trente volumes.
vwasi yn edisjɔ̃ ɑ̃ trɑ̃ːt vɔlym.
Here's an edition in thirty volumes.

11. — C'est combien?
s ɛ kɔ̃bjɛ̃?
How much is it?

12. — Six cents francs, la taxe en plus.
si sɑ̃ frɑ̃, la taks ɑ̃ ply.
Six hundred francs, not including tax.

13. — Hélas! je ne suis pas millionnaire.
elɑːs! ʒə n sɥi pɑ miljɔnɛːr.
Unfortunately I am not a millionaire.

14. — Mais, un bon livre est un trésor.
mɛ, œ̃ bɔ̃ liːvr ɛt‿œ̃ trezɔːr.
But a good book is a treasure.

le relieur [rəljœːr], *binder.* [3] **le conte** [kɔ̃ːt], *short story;* **le roman policier** [rɔmɑ̃ pɔlisje], *detective story;* **la biographie** [biɔgrafi], *biography;* **l'histoire** [listwaːr], *history.*

CHEZ LE BIJOUTIER

At the Jeweler's

1. — Regardez donc ce collier de perles!
rəgarde dɔ̃(k) sə kɔlje d(ə) pɛrl!
Just look at that pearl necklace!
2. — Et ce bracelet, que c'est beau!
e sə braslɛ, k(ə) s ɛ bo!
And how pretty that bracelet is!
3. — Moi, je n'aime pas l'émeraude. Et vous?
mwa, ʒə n ɛm pɑ l emroːd. e vu?
I don't like the emerald. Do you?
4. — Je préfère le rubis et le diamant.
ʒə prefɛːr lə rybi e l(ə) djamɑ̃.
I prefer the ruby and the diamond.
5. — Et cette bague, comment la trouvez-vous?
e sɛt bag, kɔmɑ̃ la truve vu?
And how do you like that ring?
6. — La bague en or avec les diamants?
la bag ɑ̃n‿ɔːr avɛk le djamɑ̃?
The gold ring with the diamonds?
7. — L'autre, en platine avec les saphirs.
l oːtr, ɑ̃ platin avɛk le safiːr.
The other one, platinum with sapphires.

[1] **une alliance** [aljɑ̃ːs] = **un anneau de mariage** [ano d(ə) marjaːʒ], *wedding ring;* **la breloque** [brəlɔk], *charm, trinket;* **le camée** [kame], *cameo;* **le collier** [kɔlje], *necklace;* **la montre-bracelet**

8. — Elle est ravissante, très distinguée.
ɛl ɛ ravisɑ̃ːt, trɛ distɛ̃ge.
It's charming, very elegant.

9. — Oui, mais ça doit coûter une fortune.
wi, mɛ sa dwa kute yn fɔrtyn.
Yes, but it must cost a fortune.

10. — Évidemment. Et ce pendentif?[1]
evidamɑ̃. e s(ə) pɑ̃dɑ̃tif?
Of course. And that pendant?

11. — En argent avec une turquoise?
ɑ̃n‿arʒɑ̃ avɛk yn tyrkwaːz?
The silver one with the turquoise?

12. — Oui, je crois que je vais l'acheter.
wi, ʒə krwɑ kə ʒ(ə) vɛ l aʃte.
Yes, I think I'll buy it.

13. — Moi, j'aime ces boutons à manchettes.
mwa, ʒ ɛm se butɔ̃ a mɑ̃ʃɛt.
I like those cuff links.

14. — Demandons le prix au bijoutier.
d(ə)mɑ̃dɔ̃ lə pri o biʒutje.
Let's ask the jeweler the price.

[mɔ̃ːtrbraslɛ], *wrist watch;* **la chaîne** [ʃɛːn] **de montre,** *watch chain;* **le pendant d'oreille** [pɑ̃dɑ̃ dɔrɛːj], *earring;* **le médaillon** [medajɔ̃], *medallion;* **la médaille** [medaːj], *medal.*

AU MAGASIN

At the Store (Shop)

1\. — Le rayon des mouchoirs, s.v.p.?
lə rɛjɔ̃ de muʃwaːr, . . .
The handkerchief counter, please?

2\. — En face de vous, madame, au fond.
ɑ̃ fas də vu, madam, o fɔ̃.
Facing you, madam, at the back.

3\. — (*A la vendeuse*) Vous avez des mouchoirs?
(a la vɑ̃døːz) vuz‿ave de muʃwaːr?
(To the clerk) *Have you any handkerchiefs?*

4\. — Oui, madame. Je vais vous en montrer.
wi, madam. ʒ(ə) vɛ vuz‿ɑ̃ mɔ̃tre.
Yes, (madam). I'll show you some.

5\. — Ceux-ci, c'est combien la douzaine?
sø si, s ɛ kɔ̃bjɛ̃ la duzɛn?
How much are these a dozen?

6\. — Soixante-dix francs la douzaine.
swasɑ̃ːt di frɑ̃ la duzɛn.
Seventy francs a dozen.

7\. — Ils sont beaucoup trop chers.
i(l) sɔ̃ boku tro ʃɛːr.
They are much too expensive.

[1] **la soie** [swɑ], *silk;* **le cuir** [kɥiːr], *leather;* **le velours** [v(ə)luːr], *velvet;* **le lin** [lɛ̃], *linen.*

Repeat the dialogue substituting for **mouchoirs** the following: **les bas** [bɑ], *m. pl. stockings;* **les chaussettes** [ʃosɛt], *f. pl. socks;* **les**

8. — Ils sont très bon marché, madame.
i(l) sɔ̃ trɛ bɔ̃ marʃe, madam.
They are very cheap, madam.

9. — Et ceux-là, à bordure en dentelle [1]?
e sø la, a bɔrdyːr ɑ̃ dɑ̃tɛl?
And those, with the lace border?

10. — C'est douze francs pièce.
s ɛ duːz frɑ̃ pjɛs.
Twelve francs apiece.

11. — Donnez-m'en une douzaine.
dɔne m ɑ̃ yn duzɛːn.
Give me a dozen of them.

12. — Faut-il y mettre vos initiales?
fot‿i(l) i mɛt(r) voz‿inisjal?
Do you want your initials put on them?

13. — S.v.p. Et livrez-les à domicile.
. . . e livre le a dɔmisil.
Please. And deliver them to my home.

14. — Alors il faut payer d'avance.
alɔːr i(l) fo pɛje d avɑ̃ːs.
Then it is necessary to pay in advance.

chemises [ʃmiːz], *f. pl. shirts,* etc. Note changes for feminine nouns: **ceux-ci** becomes **celles-ci** [sɛlsi], **ils** becomes **elles** [ɛl], **chers** becomes **chères** [ʃɛːr], **ceux-là** becomes **celles-là** [sɛlla], etc.; § 15.

LE MARCHÉ AUX FLEURS

The Flower Market

1. — Oh, quelles jolies fleurs!
o, kɛl ʒɔli flœːr!
Oh, what pretty flowers!
2. — Ces roses [1] sentent si bon!
se roːz sɑ̃ːt si bɔ̃!
These roses smell so sweet!
3. — Quel parfum exquis! C'est délicieux.
kɛl parfœ̃ ɛkski! s ɛ delisjø.
What a lovely fragrance! It's delightful.
4. — Regardez donc ces pois de senteur!
rəgarde dɔ̃ se pwɑ d sɑ̃tœːr!
Just look at those sweet peas!
5. — Et ces violettes! Et ce beau lilas!
e se vjɔlɛt! e sə bo lilɑ!
And those violets! And that beautiful lilac!
6. — Madame, combien le muguet?
madam, kɔ̃bjɛ̃ l(ə) mygɛ?
(Madam), how much are the lilies of the valley?
7. — Trois francs le bouquet, mademoiselle.
trwɑ frɑ̃ l(ə) bukɛ, madmwazɛl.
Three francs a bouquet, (Miss).

[1] **un œillet** [œjɛ], *carnation;* **le camélia** [kamelja], *camelia;* **le pot** [po] **de fleurs,** *potted flower;* **le pot à fleurs,** *flowerpot;* **le réséda** [rezeda], *mignonette;* **le lis** [lis], *lily;* **la giroflée** [ʒirɔfle], *stock;* **la**

8. — C'est un peu fané, il me semble.
s εt‿œ̃ pø fane, i(l) m(ə) sɑ̃ːbl.
They're a little wilted, I think.

9. — C'est frais comme la rosée.
s ε frε kɔm la roze.
They're as fresh as the dew.

10. — Et ce lilas blanc, c'est combien?
e sə lilɑ blɑ̃ s ε kɔ̃bjε̃?
And how much for that white lilac?

11. — Deux francs la branche.
dø frɑ̃ la brɑ̃ːʃ.
Two francs a branch.

12. — Donnez-moi une branche seulement.
dɔne mwa yn brɑ̃ːʃ sœlmɑ̃.
Give me only one branch.

13. — Faut-il l'envelopper, mademoiselle?
fot‿ i(l) l ɑ̃vlɔpe, madmwazεl?
Do you want it wrapped up, (Miss)?

14. — Merci. Ce n'est pas la peine.
mεrsi. sə n ε pɑ la pεn.
No, thanks. It's not worth while.

capucine [kapysin], *nasturtium;* **le myosotis** [mjɔzɔtis], *forget-me-not;* **une orchidée** [ɔrkide], *orchid;* **la violette** [vjɔlεt], *violet;* **la gerbe** [ʒεrːb], *bunch.*

POUR DEMANDER SON CHEMIN

To Ask One's Way

1. — Pardon, monsieur l'agent, où est —?
pardɔ̃, məsjø laʒɑ̃, u ɛ —?
Pardon me, (officer), where is —?
2. — Faites attention aux voitures!
fɛt(z) atɑ̃sjɔ̃ o vwatyːr!
Look out for the cars!
3. — Où est l'American Express, s.v.p.?
u ɛ l amerikan ɛksprɛs, . . .
Where is the American Express, please?
4. — Vous voulez aller à pied?
vu vule(z) ale a pje?
Do you want to walk?
5. — Oui, si ce n'est pas trop loin.
wi, si s n ɛ pɑ tro lwɛ̃.
Yes, if it's not too far.
6. — A la prochaine rue, tournez à droite.
a la prɔʃɛn ry, turne(z) a drwɑt.
At the next street turn to the right.
7. — Sur l'avenue de l'Opéra?
syr l avny d(ə) l ɔpera?
On the Avenue de l'Opéra?

[1] **en face** [ɑ̃ fas], *opposite;* **de ce côté** [də sə kote], *on this side;* **de l'autre côté** [də loːtr kote], *on the other side;* **par où va-t-on à la gare** [par u vatɔ̃ a la gaːr]? *how does one get to the station?* **est-ce bien la direction de . . .** [ɛs bjɛ̃ la dirɛksjɔ̃ də]? *is this the right way*

8. — C'est ça, et puis tout droit.
s ɛ sa, e pɥi tu drwɑ.
That's right, and then straight ahead.

9. — Près de la Place de l'Opéra?
prɛ d(ə) la plas d(ə) l ɔpera?
Near the Place de l'Opéra?

10. — Sur la Place même, à gauche.
syr la plas mɛːm, a goːʃ.
Right on the Place, to the left.

11. — Au coin [1] du Boulevard des Capucines?
o kwɛ̃ dy bulvaːr de kapysin?
On the corner of Boulevard des Capucines?

12. — Ah, non, au coin de la rue Scribe.
ɑ, nɔ̃, o kwɛ̃ d(ə) la ry skriːb.
No, on the corner of rue Scribe.

13. — Bon. Je connais le chemin. Merci.
bɔ̃. ʒ(ə) kɔnɛ l(ə) ʃmɛ̃. mɛrsi.
Fine. I know the way. Thank you.

14. — A votre service.
a vɔt(r) sɛrvis.
At your service.

to . . .? **quel est le chemin le plus court** (**le plus long**) **pour aller à** . . . [kɛl ɛ l(ə) ʃ(ə)mɛ̃ l(ə) ply kuːr (lə ply lɔ̃) pur ale a]? *what is the shortest (longest) way to go . . .?*

CHEZ LE MARCHAND D'ANTIQUITÉS [1]

At the Antique Dealer's

1. — De quel style est ce bureau [2] ?
dә kɛl stil ɛ sә byro?
What style is this desk?
2. — C'est du pur Louis quinze,[3] madame.
s ɛ dy pyr lwi kɛ̃:z, madam.
Pure Louis Quinze (XV), madam.
3. — C'est une imitation, je suppose.
s ɛt‿yn imitɑsjɔ̃, ʒ(ә) sypo:z.
It's an imitation, I suppose.
4. — Ah, non! madame. C'est authentique.
ɑ, nɔ̃! madam. s ɛt‿otɑ̃tik.
Oh, no, madam! It's authentic.
5. — Cette pendule est du même style?
sɛt pɑ̃dyl ɛ dy mɛ:m stil?
Is that clock of the same period?
6. — Non, c'est une pendule Empire.
nɔ̃, s ɛt‿yn pɑ̃dyl ɑ̃pi:r.
No, it's an Empire clock.
7. — Ces deux candélabres aussi?
se dø kɑ̃delɑ:br osi?
These two candelabra also?

[1] **un antiquaire** [œ̃n ɑ̃tikɛ:r] = **marchand d'antiquités** [marʃɑ̃ dɑ̃tikite]. [2] **le fauteuil** [fotœ:j], *armchair;* **la chaise** [ʃɛ:z], *chair;* **la commode** [kɔmɔd], *chest of drawers;* **un écran** [ekrɑ̃], *screen;* **le chenet** [ʃ(ә)nɛ], *andiron;* **le guéridon** [geridɔ̃], *stand;* **la biblio-**

8. — Oui, madame. Une très belle garniture.
wi, madam. yn trɛ bɛl garnityːr.
Yes, madam. A beautiful ornament.

9. — Et c'est combien, le tout ensemble?
e s ɛ kɔ̃bjɛ̃, lə tut ɑ̃sɑ̃ːbl?
And how much is the whole thing?

10. — Trois mille francs. Une occasion.
trwɑ mil frɑ̃. yn ɔkɑzjɔ̃.
Three thousand francs. A bargain.

11. — Mais c'est fantastique, ce prix-là!
mɛ s ɛ fɑ̃tastik, s(ə) pri la!
But that's a fabulous price!

12. — Ce sont de vrais objets d'art.
sə sɔ̃ də vrɛz‿ɔbʒɛ d aːr.
But they're real works of art.

13. — Tenez, je vous en offre deux mille.
təne, ʒ(ə) vuz‿ɑ̃n‿ɔfr dø mil.
Here, I'll give you two thousand.

14. — Puisque c'est vous, j'accepte.
pɥisk(ə) s ɛ vu, ʒ aksɛpt.
Since it's you, I'll accept.

thèque [bibliɔtɛk], *bookcase;* **une horloge** [ɔrlɔːʒ], *clock;* **le tabouret** [taburɛ], *stool;* **le secrétaire** [səkretɛːr], *writing desk, secretary;* **la vitrine** [vitrin], *glass cabinet.* [3] **Louis quatorze** [lwi katɔrz], *Louis XIV;* **Louis seize** [sɛːz], *Louis XVI.*

LA RADIO

The Radio

1. — Vous avez une radio, n'est-ce pas?
vuz‿ ave(z) yn radjo, n ɛ s pɑ?
You have a radio, haven't you?
2. — Oui. J'ai un très bon appareil.
wi. ʒ e œ̃ trɛ bɔ̃n‿aparɛːj.
Yes. I have a very good set.
3. — On peut entendre l'Amérique?
ɔ̃ pøt‿ ɑ̃tɑ̃ːdr l amerik?
Can you get America?
4. — Certainement, par ondes courtes.
sɛrtɛnmɑ̃, par ɔ̃ːd kurt.
Certainly, by short wave.
5. — Je voudrais bien écouter quelquefois.
ʒ(ə) vudrɛ bjɛ̃(n) ekute kɛlkfwa.
I should like to listen sometime.
6. — Venez donc chez moi ce soir.
vəne dɔ̃(k) ʃe mwa sə swaːr.
Do come over tonight.
7. — Entendu. A quelle heure?
ɑ̃tɑ̃dy. a kɛl œːr?
All right. At what time?

Additional words: **fermer** [fɛrme] **la radio,** *to turn off the radio;* **ça ne marche pas** [sa n marʃ pɑ], *it is out of order;* **le tabulateur** [tabylatœːr], *dial;* **régler** [regle] **sur un poste,** *to tune in a station;* **le haut-parleur** [lə o parlœːr], *loud-speaker;* **l'annonceur** [lanɔ̃sœːr]

8. — Pour l'émission de neuf heures?
pur l emisjɔ̃ d(ə) nœv œːr?
For the nine-o'clock broadcast?

9. — Quelle sorte de programme est-ce?
kɛl sɔrt d(ə) prɔgram ɛ s?
What kind of program is it?

10. — Les nouvelles du jour.
le nuvɛl dy ʒuːr.
The latest news.

11. — La réception est assez claire?
la resɛpsjɔ̃ ɛt‿ase klɛːr?
Is the reception clear?

12. — Oui, mais ça dépend des jours.
wi, mɛ sa depɑ̃ de ʒuːr.
Yes, but that depends on the day.

13. — Quel poste écoutez-vous?
kɛl pɔst ekute vu?
Which station do you listen to?

14. — Radio City. Un poste excellent.
Radjo siti. œ̃ pɔst ɛksɛlɑ̃.
Radio City. An excellent station.

or **le speaker** [spikeːr], *announcer;* **faites marcher** [fɛt marʃe] **la radio,** *turn on the radio;* **détraqué** [detrake], *out of order;* **les parasites** [parazit], *static;* **syntoniser (capter)** [sɛ̃tɔnize (kapte)], *to tune in* (to a station).

L'OPÉRA

The Opera

1. — Vous aimez l'opéra, n'est-ce pas?
vuz‿ ɛme l ɔpera, n ɛ s pɑ?
You like opera, don't you?
2. — Ah, j'adore la musique et le chant!
ɑ, ʒ adɔːr la myzik e l(ə) ʃɑ̃!
Oh, I love the music and the singing!
3. — On joue « Faust » demain soir.
ɔ̃ ʒu fost dmɛ̃ swaːr.
They're playing "Faust" tomorrow evening.
4. — Je voudrais bien voir ça.
ʒ(ə) vudrɛ bjɛ̃ vwaːr sa.
I should like to see that.
5. — J'ai deux fauteuils d'orchestre.[1]
ʒ e dø fotœːj d ɔrkɛstr.
I have two orchestra seats.
6. — Un pour moi! Comme vous êtes gentil!
œ̃ pur mwa! kɔm vuz‿ɛt ʒɑ̃ti!
One for me! You're very kind!
7. — On se met en tenue de soirée?
ɔ̃ s(ə) mɛt‿ɑ̃ tny d(ə) sware?
Are we going to wear evening clothes?

[1] **une loge** [lɔːʒ], *box;* **une boîte (de nuit)** [bwat d nɥi], *night club.* [2] **ténor** [tenɔːr], *tenor;* **basse** [bɑːs], *bass;* **soprano** [sɔprano], *soprano.* [3] Future, § 35, I.

Additional vocabulary: **le rang** [rɑ̃], *row;* **le livret** [livrɛ], *libretto;*

8. — Pas en habit, en smoking.
pɑ(z) ɑ̃n‿abi, ɑ̃ smɔkiɲ.
Not full dress, a Tuxedo.

9. — Si vous voulez. C'est très correct.
si vu vule. s ɛ trɛ kɔrɛkt.
If you wish. It's perfectly proper.

10. — Qui joue le rôle de Marguerite?
ki ʒu lə roːl d(ə) margərit?
Who plays the role of Marguerite?

11. — Une nouvelle vedette [2] russe, je crois.
yn nuvɛl vədɛt rys, ʒ(ə) krwɑ.
A new Russian star, I believe.

12. — Espérons qu'elle a une bonne voix.
ɛsperɔ̃ k ɛl a yn bɔn vwɑ.
Let's hope she has a good voice.

13. — La distribution est excellente.
la distribysjɔ̃ ɛt‿ɛksɛlɑ̃ːt.
The cast is excellent.

14. — Nous passerons [3] une soirée charmante.
nu pɑsrɔ̃ yn sware ʃarmɑ̃ːt.
We'll have a charming evening.

siffler [sifle], *to hiss;* **la répétition** [repetisjɔ̃], *rehearsal;* **la reprise** [rəpriːz], *revival;* **les décors** [dekɔːr], *m. pl. scenery;* **les jumelles** [ʒymɛl], *f. pl. opera glasses.*

A LA PHARMACIE

At the Drugstore

1. — Bonjour, monsieur. Vous désirez?
   bɔ̃ʒuːr, məsjø. vu dezire?
   How do you do, sir. What did you wish?
2. — J'ai une ordonnance du médecin.
   ʒ e yn ɔrdɔnɑ̃ːs dy medsɛ̃.
   I have a doctor's prescription.
3. — Bien. On va vous la préparer.
   bjɛ̃. ɔ̃ va vu la prepare.
   All right. We'll fill it for you.
4. — Vous avez de la pâte dentifrice?
   vuz‿ave d(ə) la pɑːt dɑ̃tifris?
   Have you tooth paste?
5. — Certainement. Voici une bonne marque.
   sɛrtɛnmɑ̃. vwasi yn bɔn mark.
   Certainly. Here is a good brand.
6. — J'ai besoin d'une brosse à dents.
   ʒ e bəzwɛ̃ d yn brɔs a dɑ̃.
   I need a toothbrush.
7. — Je vous recommande celle-ci.
   ʒ(ə) vu rəkɔmɑ̃ːd sɛl si.
   I recommend this one.

Useful words: **le pharmacien** [farmasjɛ̃], *pharmacist;* **la quinine** [kinin], *quinine;* **le thermomètre** [tɛrmɔmɛtr], *thermometer;* **la blessure** [blɛsyːr], *wound;* **le bandage** [bɑ̃daːʒ], *bandage;* **le cachet d'aspirine** [kaʃɛ daspirin], *aspirin tablet;* **le bicarbonate** [bikar-

8. — Et un flacon de teinture d'iode.
e œ̃ flakɔ̃ d(ə) tɛ̃tyːr d jɔd.
And a little bottle of tincture of iodine.

9. — Oui, monsieur. Et avec cela?
wi, məsjø. e avɛk sla?
Yes, sir. And what else (lit. 'with that')?

10. — Oh, quelque chose pour la toux.
o, kɛlk ʃoːz pur la tu.
Oh, something for a cough.

11. — Ces pastilles sont très efficaces.
se pastiːj sɔ̃ trɛz‿ɛfikas.
These cough drops are very effective.

12. — Bien. Je crois que c'est tout.
bjɛ̃. ʒ(ə) krwɑ k(ə) s ɛ tu.
All right. I think that's all.

13. — Voilà. Tout est dans ce paquet.
vwala. tut‿ ɛ dɑ̃ sə pakɛ.
There you are. Everything's in this package.

14. — Merci bien. Bonjour, monsieur.
mɛrsi bjɛ̃. bɔ̃ʒuːr, məsjø.
Thank you. Good day, (sir).

bɔnat], *bicarbonate;* **la capsule** [kapsyl], *capsule;* **un rhume de cerveau** [rym d(ə) sɛrvo], *head cold;* **rhume de poitrine** [pwatrin], *chest cold;* **être enrhumé** [ɑ̃ryme], *to have a cold;* **souffrir de l'estomac** [sufrir d(ə) lɛstɔma], etc., *to have stomach trouble,* etc.

PART II

UNE PARTIE DE CARTES

A Game of Cards

1. — Voulez-vous faire une partie de cartes avec Jeanne et moi?
2. — Je veux bien, mais comment? Nous ne sommes que trois.
3. — Qu'est-ce que ça fait? On fera un mort.
4. — Alors, tirons au sort pour voir qui fera la donne.
5. — A vous. C'est vous qui avez la carte la plus haute.
6. — Voilà. Les cartes sont battues. Voulez-vous couper?
7. — C'est fait. Allez-y.
8. — Qui est-ce qui peut ouvrir?
9. — Je passe.
10. — A vous de jouer.
11. — Pourquoi avez-vous joué atout avec votre roi de trèfle? [1]
12. — C'est bien simple. C'est parce que je ne pouvais pas jouer dans la couleur.
13. — A vous. Ça va bien. Nous avons déjà gagné deux manches.
14. — Combien de points avons-nous?

49

1. Would you like to play a game of cards with Jean and myself?
2. I'd be glad to, but how? There are only three of us.
3. What difference does it make? We'll have a dummy.
4. Then let's draw to see who deals.
5. You deal. You have the highest card.
6. There. The cards are shuffled. Do you want to cut?
7. It's done. Go ahead.
8. Who can open?
9. I pass.
10. It's your play.
11. Why did you trump with your king of clubs?
12. It's very simple. Because I couldn't follow suit.
13. It's your play. We are doing fine. We've already won two hands.
14. What's the score (lit. 'How many points have we')?

15. —Je ne sais pas. Mais nous avons tous les honneurs.

[1] **le roi,** *king;* **la reine,** *queen;* **le valet,** *jack;* **l'as,** *ace;* **un jeu de cartes,** *deck of cards;* **une levée,** *trick;* **tricher,** *to cheat;* **un partenaire,** *partner;* **un adversaire,** *opponent;* **c'est à refaire,** *we must have another deal;* **quel est l'atout?** *what are trumps?* **couper avec un**

LE FOOTBALL

Football

1. —On joue au [1] football dimanche prochain au stade Pershing.
2. —Oui, je sais. J'ai vu l'annonce dans le journal.
3. —Si on y allait? Qu'est-ce que vous en dites?
4. —Moi, j'irai volontiers. Qui est-ce qui joue?
5. —C'est une équipe anglaise contre une équipe française.
6. —Alors ça va être un jeu très animé.
7. —Pour sûr. Je me demande quelle équipe va gagner.
8. —On dit que les Français sont très bien entraînés.[2]
9. —C'est possible. Mais les Anglais ont gagné de belles victoires cette saison.

15. I don't know. But we have all the honors.

atout, *to trump;* **une séquence,** *sequence;* **à qui de donner?** *whose deal is it?* **à vous la donne!** *your deal!* **une maldonne,** *misdeal;* **le cœur,** *heart;* **le carreau,** *diamond;* **le trêfle,** *club;* **le pique,** *spade.*

50

1. There's going to be a football game next Sunday at the Pershing Stadium.
2. Yes, I know. I saw the announcement in the paper.
3. How about going? What do you say?
4. I'll be glad to go. Who's playing?
5. An English team against a French team.
6. Well, that'll be a very lively game.
7. It surely will. I wonder which team will win.
8. They say the French are very well trained.
9. That's possible. But the English have won some fine victories this season.

10. — N'oubliez pas que les Français les ont battus [3] il y a un an.
11. — Je sais. Mais depuis ils ont perdu leurs meilleurs joueurs.
12. — C'est égal [4]; je suis sûr que les Français gagneront cette fois.
13. — Oui? Alors, combien voulez-vous parier?
14. — Deux contre un. Et vous avez perdu d'avance.

[1] **jouer *à*** (games), **jouer *de*** (musical instruments); **jouez-vous du piano?** *do you play the piano?* [2] **entraîneur,** *coach;* **le ballon,**

LE TENNIS

Tennis

1. — Est-ce que vous aimez jouer au tennis?
2. — Oui, beaucoup; mais je joue très mal.
3. — Voilà un court (de tennis) qui me semble excellent.
4. — En effet. Et il est marqué pour les jeux simples et doubles.
5. — Arrêtons-nous un instant pour regarder ces jeunes gens.
6. — Voyez comme cette jeune fille est souple (agile).

10. Don't forget that the French beat them a year ago.
11. I know. But since then they have lost their best players.
12. That doesn't matter; I'm sure the French will win this time.
13. Yes? Then how much will you bet?
14. Two to one. And you've already lost (lit. 'you've lost in advance').

ball. [3] from **battre,** § 40. [4] **cela (ça) m'est égal,** *I don't care, it's all the same to me.*

51

1. Do you like to play tennis?
2. Yes, very much; but I play very badly.
3. That seems to be an excellent (tennis) court.

4. (Yes) indeed. It's marked for singles and doubles.
5. Let's stop a minute to watch these young people.

6. See how nimble (agile) that girl is.

7. — Et elle sert [1] avec beaucoup d'adresse.
8. — La balle rase tout juste le filet.
9. — Mais le jeu de ce garçon n'est pas moins admirable.
10. — N'est-ce pas? Et son coup de revers est épatant.
11. — Voulez-vous jouer une partie avec moi demain matin?
12. — Je veux bien. Mais je vous avertis que je suis un joueur médiocre.
13. — Vous êtes trop modeste. N'oubliez pas d'apporter la raquette et les balles.
14. — Je n'oublierai rien, pas même les souliers blancs et les pantalons de flanelle.

[1] **à quoi sert cela?** *what is that used for?* **de quoi vous servez-vous pour écrire?** *what do you use to write with?*

Additional sports vocabulary: **la barre fixe,** *horizontal bar;* **la boxe,** *boxing;* **la chasse,** *hunting;* **la course,** *race;* **l'escrime** *f.*

AU BUREAU DE TABAC

At the Tobacco Shop

1. — Bonjour, monsieur. Vous désirez?
2. — Vous avez des cigarettes américaines (turques)?

7. And she's very clever at serving.
8. The ball just grazes the net.
9. But that boy's game is just as fine.

10. Isn't it? And his backhand stroke is marvelous.

11. Will you play a game with me tomorrow morning?
12. Glad to. But I warn you that I'm only a mediocre player.
13. You're too modest. Don't forget to bring the racket and the balls.
14. I shan't forget a thing, not even my white shoes and my flannel trousers.

fencing; **en faveur de,** *in favor of;* **la glace,** *ice;* **la lutte,** *wrestling;* **la marche,** *hiking;* **la natation,** *swimming;* **nager,** *to swim;* **le patin,** *skate;* **le patinage,** *skating;* **patiner,** *to skate;* **la piscine,** *swimming pool;* **la piste,** *track;* **le terrain,** *field.*

52

1. Good morning, sir. What would you like?
2. Do you have any American (Turkish) cigarettes?

3. — Oui, monsieur. Nous avons plusieurs marques étrangères.
4. — Donnez-moi un paquet d'*Excel*. Je n'aime pas le tabac français.
5. — Ah, ça, c'est affaire de goût. Et avec ça, monsieur?
6. — Dites-moi, c'est combien, cette pipe en écume de mer?
7. — Deux cents francs. C'est une occasion.
8. — Même alors c'est trop cher. Et ce briquet?
9. — Cent vingt francs. Il est garanti. Pluie ou vent, il ne rate jamais.
10. — J'ai plus grande confiance dans les allumettes. Donnez-moi une boîte de suédoises.
11. — L'État [1] ne les garantit pas, vous savez.
12. — Je sais, mais au moins on en a pour son argent. Donnez-moi aussi deux timbres pour l'étranger, s.v.p.
13. — Oui, monsieur. Et cet étui à cigarettes,[2] ça ne vous intéresse pas?
14. — Non, merci. J'en ai un très bon. C'est tout pour aujourd'hui.

[1] In France, tobacco and matches are a state monopoly and are sold at the **bureau de tabac,** where stamps are likewise available, singly and in booklets (**un carnet de timbres**). Barmen sell light

3. Yes, sir. We have several foreign brands.

4. Give me a package of *Excel*. I don't like French tobacco.
5. Well, that's a matter of taste. And what else, sir?
6. Tell me, how much is that meerschaum pipe?

7. Two hundred francs. It's a bargain.
8. Even at that it's too expensive. And this lighter?
9. A hundred and twenty francs. It's guaranteed. Rain or wind, it never misses (never fails to light).
10. I have more confidence in matches. Give me a box of safety matches (lit. 'Swedish matches').
11. The government doesn't guarantee them, you know.
12. I know, but at least you get a lot for your money. Give me also two stamps for foreign countries, please.
13. Yes, sir. Doesn't this cigarette case interest you?
14. No, thank you. I have a very good one. That's all for today.

drinks both on the sidewalk and at tables within. [2] **un porte-cigarette,** *a cigarette holder*.

CHEZ LE DENTISTE[1]

At the Dentist's

1. — Vous avez mal aux dents? Laquelle vous fait mal?
2. — Celle-ci, cette molaire dans la mâchoire supérieure, à gauche.
3. — Depuis quand vous fait-elle mal?
4. — Depuis plusieurs jours, mais je ne souffrais pas beaucoup.
5. — Et maintenant, vous souffrez davantage?
6. — J'ai un mal terrible. Je n'ai pas dormi toute la nuit.
7. — Cette dent est cariée. Et il y a peut-être un commencement d'abcès.
8. — Aïe! vous me faites mal, docteur. Vous avez touché le nerf.
9. — Je pourrai peut-être la sauver. Mais il faut d'abord la radiographier.[2]
10. — Vous croyez qu'il ne sera pas nécessaire de l'arracher?
11. — J'espère que non. On verra.
12. — Alors, il suffira de la plomber,[3] n'est-ce pas?
13. — Oui. Revenez me voir demain, à la même heure.
14. — Mais en attendant j'aurai toujours mal?

53

1. Do you have a toothache? Which one hurts?
2. This one, this molar in the upper jaw, on the left.
3. How long has it been aching?
4. For several days, but I wasn't suffering much.
5. And now you're suffering more?
6. I have a terrible pain. I didn't sleep all night.
7. That tooth is decayed. And there's probably an incipient abscess.
8. Oh! You're hurting me, Doctor. You hit the nerve.
9. Perhaps I'll be able to save it. But we'll have to take an X ray first.
10. You think it won't be necessary to extract it?
11. I hope not. We shall see.
12. In that case, a filling will do, won't it (lit. 'it will suffice to fill it')?
13. Yes. Come back to see me tomorrow, at the same time.
14. But meanwhile will it continue to hurt me?

15. — Mais non. Ce médicament vous empêchera de souffrir.[4]

[1] **cabinet du dentiste,** *dentist's office;* **heures de consultation,** *office hours;* **à quelle heure pourriez-vous me donner une consultation ?** *at what time could you give me an appointment?* [2] **radio-**

CHEZ LA COUTURIÈRE

At the Dressmaker's

1. — Bonjour. Vous voyez comme je suis ponctuelle.
2. — En effet, madame. Veuillez attendre un instant. J'ai à m'occuper d'un autre essayage.
3. — Je ne suis pas pressée. En attendant je vais regarder ces dessins.
4. — (*Après un moment*) Je suis à vous, madame. Voici votre robe.[1] Voulez-vous bien l'essayer ?
5. — Il me semble que le corsage est trop large. Ne trouvez-vous pas ?
6. — Je ne trouve pas. Mais on pourrait serrer un peu la taille.[2]
7. — C'est ça. Baissez la taille par devant et relevez-la dans le dos.

15. No, indeed. This medicine will keep you from suffering.

graphie, *f. X ray.* [3] **plombage,** *m. filling.* [4] **anesthésier,** *to anesthetize;* **gencives,** *f. pl. gums;* **fausses dents,** *false teeth.*

54

1. Good afternoon. I'm very punctual, as you see.

2. You certainly are, (madam). Will you kindly wait a minute? I'm busy with another fitting.
3. I'm not in a hurry. While I'm waiting, I'll look at these designs.
4. (*After a short while*) I'm ready for you now. This is your dress. Do you mind trying it on?

5. It seems to be too full through the bust. Don't you think?
6. No, I don't. But it could be taken in a bit at the waist.
7. That's right. Make the waist lower in front and higher in back.

8. — Comment trouvez-vous les manches? Levez les bras.
9. — Elles sont trop étroites. Elles me gênent sous l'aisselle.
10. — Bien, je vais les élargir. Le col est parfait. Les épaules sont très bien aussi. Il n'y a rien à changer.
11. — La robe tombe bien du côté droit, mais elle n'est pas égale du côté gauche.
12. — Je vais l'épingler comme il faut. Les corrections seront vite faites.
13. — Vous savez, je tiens beaucoup à la porter demain soir.
14. — Soyez tranquille. Elle vous sera livrée sans manque dans l'après-midi.

[1] robe décolletée, *low-neck dress;* robe de soirée, *evening dress;* se mettre en robe de soirée pour dîner, *to dress for dinner.* [2] long

ARTICLES DE PHOTOGRAPHIE

Photographic Supplies

1. — Est-ce que vous avez développé mes pellicules?
2. — Oui, mademoiselle. Voici vos négatifs. Et voilà les épreuves.

8. How do you like the sleeves? Raise your arms.

9. They're too narrow. They're too tight under the arms (lit. 'armpit').
10. All right, I'll let them out. The collar is perfect. The shoulders are fine, too. There's nothing to be altered.
11. The dress hangs well on the right side, but it's uneven on the left side.
12. I'll pin it up as it should be. The alterations will be quickly made.
13. You know I'm very anxious to wear it tomorrow evening.
14. Don't worry. It will be delivered to you without fail in the afternoon.

(longue) de taille, *long-waisted;* **court (courte) de taille,** *short-waisted;* **prend bien la taille,** *is close-fitting.*

55

1. Have you developed my films?

2. Yes, (Miss). Here are your negatives. And there are the proofs.

3. — Comment? Il n'y a que quatre sur six de réussi?
4. — En effet. Un des clichés est trop exposé et l'autre n'est pas au point.
5. — J'ai pourtant un bon appareil et un objectif très fin.
6. — Vous n'avez pas eu de chance, mademoiselle. Cela peut arriver à tout le monde.
7. — Ah, voilà un cliché qui est très net. Pouvez-vous en faire un agrandissement?
8. — Mais certainement. Quelle dimension? Huit (centimètres) sur dix?
9. — Bien. Et tirez-en deux épreuves, une sur papier glacé et l'autre sur papier mat.
10. — Entendu. Avez-vous essayé de faire de la photo-cinéma, mademoiselle?
11. — Non, ça ne m'intéresse pas. C'est trop compliqué.
12. — Pas du tout, et nous serions très heureux de vous faire une démonstration.
13. — Pensez donc! Il faut un ciné-kodak, un projecteur, des films . . . et je ne sais quoi encore!
14. — Les films en couleur sont si attrayants!
15. — Oui, mais ça coûte les yeux de la tête.
16. — Mais non, c'est très raisonnable.
17. — Merci. J'y réfléchirai.

[1] **faire tirer sa photographie** (*or* **se faire photographier**), *to have one's picture taken;* **le photographe,** *photographer;* **faire de la photo-**

3. What? Only four out of six turned out well?

4. That's right. One of the negatives is over-exposed and the other isn't in focus.
5. Still I have a good camera and a very sharp lens.

6. You had no luck, (Miss). That can happen to anyone.
7. Oh, there's a negative that's very clear. Can you make an enlargement of it?
8. Certainly. What size? Eight (centimeters) by ten?
9. Yes. And make two prints, one with a glossy finish and the other dull.
10. Very well. Have you ever tried to make moving pictures, (Miss)?
11. No, that doesn't interest me. It's too complicated.
12. Not at all, and we'd be very happy to give you a demonstration.
13. Imagine! You need a movie camera, a projector, films . . . and who knows what else!
14. Color films are so attractive!
15. Yes, but they're terribly expensive.
16. Why no, they are very reasonable.
17. Thanks. I'll think about it.

graphie, *to go in for photography.*

LA BICYCLETTE

The Bicycle

1. — C'est à vous cette bicyclette? Elle est toute neuve.
2. — Oui, je viens de l'acheter. Comment la trouvez-vous?
3. — Moi, vous savez, je ne m'y connais pas beaucoup.
4. — Je vous assure que c'est une bonne bécane. Essayez-la.
5. — La selle est trop haute. Je peux à peine toucher les pédales.
6. — On peut la baisser. On peut aussi baisser ou relever le guidon, à volonté.
7. — Qu'est-ce que c'est que cette manette? C'est pour le frein? [1]
8. — Oui, c'est pour le frein de secours. Mais on freine aussi avec les pédales.
9. — Vous savez, je n'ai plus l'habitude de monter à bicyclette.
10. — Oh, ça ne s'oublie pas. Pourquoi n'en achèteriez-vous pas une, comme moi?
11. — Ah, non. Mais je pourrais en louer une de temps en temps.
12. — C'est parfait. On pourra ainsi faire de belles tournées à la campagne.

56

1. Is that bicycle yours? It's very new.
2. Yes, I've just bought it. How do you like it?
3. You see, I don't know much about them.
4. I can assure you it's a good "bike." Try it.
5. The seat is too high. I can hardly touch the pedals.
6. It can be lowered. You can also lower or raise the handlebars to suit yourself.
7. What is this handle? Is it for the brake?
8. Yes, it's the emergency brake. You can also put on the brake with the pedals.
9. You know, I'm out of practice at riding a bicycle.
10. Oh, you don't forget that. Why don't you buy one, as I have done?
11. Oh, no. But I could rent one occasionally.
12. Fine. Then we can take some nice trips into the country.

13. — Comment sont les routes dans les environs? Pas trop de côtes?

14. — Les routes sont excellentes. On pourra pédaler à cœur joie.

[1] **le boulon,** *nut;* **serrer,** *to tighten;* **desserrer,** *to loosen;* **la chaîne,** *chain;* **le timbre,** *bell;* **la lampe,** *light;* **gonfler,** *to inflate,*

EN AUTOMOBILE (*a*)

Motoring (a)

1. — Zut! nous serons bientôt à court d'essence![1]
2. — Eh bien, ce ne sera pas drôle d'avoir une panne ici.
3. — Il nous reste à peine un litre.
4. — Ralentissez. Il y a un poste d'essence devant nous.
5. — Quelle chance! Juste à temps. (*L'auto s'arrête*)
6. — (*A l'employé*) Faites le plein, s'il vous plaît. Et vérifiez le niveau d'huile.[2]
7. — (*L'employé*) Oui, monsieur. Et votre radiateur,[3] faut-il y mettre de l'eau?
8. — Merci. Je l'ai fait remplir avant de quitter Paris.
9. — Nos pneus sont en bon état, n'est-ce pas?

13. How are the roads around here? Not too many hills?
14. The roads are excellent. You can "bike" to your heart's content.

blow up; **la pompe,** *pump;* **la clé anglaise,** *monkey wrench.*

57

1. Hang it all, we'll soon be out of gas!
2. Well, it won't be funny to get stuck here.

3. We barely have a liter left.
4. Slow down. There's a gas station ahead of us.

5. What luck! Just in time. (*The car stops*)

6. (*To the attendant*) Fill it up, please. And check the oil.
7. (*Attendant*) Yes, sir. How about the radiator; does it need water?
8. No, thank you. I had it filled before leaving Paris.
9. Our tires are in good condition, aren't they?

10. — Je crois que oui. Mais je ferai vérifier la pression d'air.
11. — Ce ne serait pas amusant d'avoir un plat [4] en route.
12. — Soyez tranquille. Nous avons un bon pneu de rechange.
13. — Et puis, ne conduisez pas si vite. La route est humide et on peut déraper.
14. — N'ayez pas peur. Quand je suis au volant, il n'y a pas de danger.

[1] **donner de l'essence**, *to give it gas.* [2] **huile lourde (moyenne, légère)**, *heavy (medium, light) oil.* [3] **fuir (avoir une fuite)**, *to leak.*

EN AUTOMOBILE (*b*)

Motoring (*b*)

1. — Ça y est. Tout est prêt. On peut repartir.
2. — Combien de kilomètres [1] nous reste-t-il à faire?
3. — Une centaine. On arrivera à temps pour dîner.
4. — Il commence à faire nuit. Il faudrait allumer les phares (mettre les lumières).[2]
5. — En effet; je ne voudrais pas tomber sur une charrette à bœufs.

10. I think so. But I'll have the air pressure checked.

11. It wouldn't be much fun to have a flat tire along the way.
12. Don't worry. We have a good spare (tire).

13. Furthermore, don't drive so fast. The road is wet and we might skid.
14. Don't be afraid. When I am at the wheel, there's no danger.

[4] **gonfler,** *to fill (with air);* **dégonfler,** *to deflate.*

58

1. All right! Everything's ready. We can start (out) again.
2. How many kilometers do we still have to go?

3. About a hundred. We'll arrive in time for dinner.
4. It's beginning to get dark. We ought to put on our lights.
5. Sure enough; I wouldn't want to collide with (lit. 'fall upon') an oxcart.

6. — Et ces paysans conduisent toujours du mauvais côté.
7. — Mais la route est bonne. On peut gazer.
8. — La côte est raide. Vous ne pourrez jamais la monter en prise directe.
9. — Si, mais je passerai en deuxième pour ne pas fatiguer le moteur.[3]
10. — Regardez donc ce poteau indicateur: Descente rapide. Tournant brusque.[4]
11. — Oui, oui, je vois. Je ferai bien attention.
12. — Voilà une voiture qui vient. Cornez ! [5]
13. — Ces feux sont aveuglants. Et cet idiot-là fait du cent à l'heure ! [6]
14. — On devrait bien lui retirer son permis de conduire.

[1] One kilometer = $\frac{5}{8}$ of a mile; 100 kilometers = $62\frac{1}{2}$ miles. [2] **baisser les phares,** *to dim the lights;* **feu pilote** *m. taillight.* [3] **caler le moteur,** *to shut off the motor.* [4] Additional signs: **Danger,** *Danger;* **Ralentir,** *Go Slow;* **Tenez Votre Droite,** *Keep to the Right;* **Tournant**

EN AUTOMOBILE (*c*)

Motoring (*c*)

1. — Ralentissez ! nous entrons dans un village.
2. — Tiens ! pourquoi tout ce monde au bord de la route ?

6. And these peasants always drive on the wrong side.
7. But the road is good. We can speed up.
8. The hill is steep. You'll never be able to make it in high (gear).
9. Yes, I would, but I'll shift into second so as not to strain the motor.
10. Just look at that signpost: Steep Incline. Sharp Turn.
11. Yes, I see. I'll be very careful.
12. Here comes a car. Blow your horn!
13. Those lights are blinding. And that idiot is going a hundred (kilometers) an hour.
14. They ought to take his driver's license away from him.

Dangereux, *Dangerous Curve.* [5] **cornez! = sonnez le klaxon!** [6] **la vitesse,** *speed;* **faire de la vitesse,** *to speed;* **indicateur de vitesse,** *speedometer.*

59

1. Slow up! We're entering a village.
2. Look! Why are all those people at the side of the road?

3. — Je parie que c'est un accident.
4. — Si on s'arrêtait ?[1] On pourra peut-être rendre service.
5. — (*A un spectateur*) Qu'est-ce qui est arrivé ?
6. — (*Le premier spectateur*) Il paraît qu'ils ont été tamponnés[2] par un camion.
7. — Il y a eu des victimes ?
8. — (*Le premier spectateur*) Les deux passagers, un monsieur et une dame, ont été blessés.
9. — (*Le deuxième spectateur*) On vient de les transporter à l'hôpital.
10. — (*Le premier spectateur*) Heureusement que personne n'a été tué.
11. — La voiture doit être bien abîmée.
12. — (*Le deuxième spectateur*) Une roue avant est arrachée, un ressort cassé, le radiateur défoncé.[3]
13. — (*Le premier spectateur*) Ça, ce n'est rien. Moi, je suis mécanicien. Je peux remettre tout ça à neuf.
14. — Je parie que c'est la même voiture qui nous a doublés à toute vitesse.
15. — Ça ne m'étonnerait pas.
16. — Vous voyez, c'est toujours dangereux de faire de la vitesse.
17. — Oui. Il faut être très prudent.

[1] Imperfect indicative of **s'arrêter,** *to stop.* [2] **culbuter,** *to overturn.*
[3] **le garde-crotte,** *mudguard;* **le marche-pied,** *running board;* **le**

3. I'll bet it's an accident.
4. Suppose we stop. Perhaps we could be of some help.
5. (*To an onlooker*) What happened?
6. (*The first bystander*) They seem to have been bumped into by a truck.
7. Was anyone hurt (lit. 'Were there any victims')?
8. (*The first bystander*) The two passengers, a man and a woman, were injured.
9. (*The second spectator*) They have just been taken to the hospital.
10. (*The first spectator*) Luckily no one was killed.

11. The car must be pretty well damaged.
12. (*The second spectator*) A front wheel was torn off, a spring broken, and the radiator smashed in.

13. (*The first spectator*) That's nothing. I'm a mechanic. I can fix all that up like new.

14. I'll bet it's the same car that passed us at top speed.
15. I wouldn't be surprised.
16. You see, it is always dangerous to speed.

17. Yes. One must be very careful.

pare-brise, *windshield;* **un essuie-glace,** *windshield wiper;* **un engrenage,** *gear;* **une courroie,** *belt.*

EN AUTOMOBILE (*d*)

Motoring (*d*)

1. — Nous avons déjà parcouru plus de trente mille kilomètres.
2. — Oui, et notre auto a besoin d'être complètement revisée.
3. — D'abord il faudra la faire graisser.
4. — Et puis les bougies devraient être nettoyées.[1]
5. — Les freins ne tiennent pas très bien non plus.
6. — Non, il faudra les faire resserrer.
7. — Comment est la chambre à air du pneu de secours ?
8. — Elle est toute rapiécée. Il faudra en acheter une neuve.
9. — Attention ! Pas par là. La rue est barrée.
10. — Zut ! Et celle-là est à sens unique.

11. — Arrêtez. Je vais descendre acheter des cigarettes.
12. — Je ne peux pas stationner ici. Il y a une bouche à incendie.
13. — Alors, avancez un peu plus loin.
14. — Si j'attrape une contravention, ce sera de votre faute !

[1] **roder les soupapes,** *to grind the valves;* **le cric,** *jack;* **un accu (accumulateur),** *battery;* **un arbre de transmission,** *axle;* **un écrou,**

60

1. We've already traveled more than thirty thousand kilometers.
2. Yes, and our car needs a complete overhauling.

3. First of all it will have to be greased.
4. And then the spark plugs ought to be cleaned.
5. The brakes aren't holding very well either.
6. No, they'll have to be tightened.
7. How is the inner tube of the spare tire?

8. It's all patches. We'll have to buy a new one.

9. Look out! Not that way. The road is closed.
10. Hang it all! And that one there is a one-way street.
11. Stop. I'm going to get out and buy some cigarettes.
12. I can't park here. There's a fire hydrant.

13. Then go on a bit farther.
14. If I get a ticket, it'll be your fault!

nut; **un outil** [uti], *tool;* **le tournevis** [turnəvis], *screwdriver;* **la vis** [vis], *screw.*

LA PLAGE

The Seashore

1. — Où comptez-vous passer vos vacances? [1]
2. — J'irai probablement dans les Alpes. J'adore la montagne.
3. — Moi, je préfère la plage. Je compte passer quelques semaines à Deauville.
4. — Je n'aime pas la mer. L'eau est trop froide. Et puis je ne sais pas nager.[2]
5. — L'eau est un peu froide, c'est vrai. Mais on se réchauffe au soleil.
6. — Je ne supporte pas les bains de soleil. Je brûle trop facilement.[3]
7. — C'est dommage. Moi, au contraire, j'aime donner un bon hâle à ma peau.
8. — Ce qui me convient le mieux, c'est un petit coin tranquille à la campagne.
9. — Deauville est très mondain. On s'y amuse beaucoup. Moi, j'aime cette vie-là.
10. — On y va moins pour prendre des bains de mer que pour jouer au casino.
11. — Il est certain que le casino offre beaucoup d'attractions: bal, musique, jeu.
12. — Vous allez sans doute vous installer à l'hôtel?
13. — Non, j'ai loué une petite villa au bord de la mer.

1. Where do you plan to spend your vacation?
2. I'll probably go to the Alps. I love the mountains.
3. I prefer the seashore. I expect to spend a few weeks at Deauville.
4. I don't like the ocean. The water is too cold. And then I don't know how to swim.
5. The water is a little cold, that's true. But one gets warmed up again in the sun.
6. I can't stand sun baths. I burn too easily.

7. That's too bad. I, on the contrary, like to get a good tan (lit. 'give a good tan to my skin').
8. What suits me best is a little quiet nook in the country.
9. Deauville is very fashionable. You can have a lot of fun there. I like that kind of life.
10. People go there not so much for sea bathing as for gambling at the Casino.
11. The Casino certainly offers many attractions: dancing, music, gambling.
12. No doubt you are going to stop at the hotel?
13. No, I've rented a cottage (small villa) right on the shore.

14. — Eh bien, je vous souhaite de bonnes vacances.

[1] **être en villégiature,** *to be vacationing* (in the country, at the seashore, or in the mountains). [2] **nageur,** *swimmer;* **patauger,** *to splash about;* **plonger,** *to dive;* **le plongeon,** *dive;* **le costume de bain,**

POUR LOUER UNE VILLA

Renting a Villa

1. — Je voudrais louer une villa pour la saison d'été.
2. — En montagne ou au bord de la mer?
3. — J'aimerais une plage tranquille, vous savez, un bon petit coin pour familles.
4. — Combien de pièces vous faudrait-il?
5. — Il nous faudrait au moins six pièces: deux chambres à coucher, une salle à manger, un salon, une cuisine et une petite chambre pour la bonne.
6. — Nous avons une jolie villa à Étretat qui fera justement votre affaire.
7. — A quelle distance se trouve-t-elle de la plage?
8. — C'est tout près, avec une vue splendide sur la Manche.
9. — La villa est complètement meublée, bien entendu?

14. Well, I hope you have a nice vacation.

bathing suit; **la brassée,** *swimming stroke;* **la douche,** *shower (bath);* **la serviette de bain,** *bath towel.* [3] **attraper un coup de soleil** (*or* **une insolation**), *to have a sunstroke;* **basané,** *tanned.*

62

1. I'd like to rent a villa for the summer season.
2. In the mountains or at the seashore?
3. I'd like a very quiet beach, you know, a nice little family spot.
4. How many rooms would you need?
5. We'd need at least six rooms: two bedrooms, a dining room, a living room, a kitchen, and a small room for the maid.

6. We have a nice villa at Étretat which will just suit you.
7. How far is it from the beach?
8. It's very close, with a fine view of the Channel.

9. The villa is completely furnished, of course?

10. — Complètement, sauf le linge et l'argenterie que vous aurez vous-même à fournir.
11. — Et quelle sorte d'installation y a-t-il?
12. — Il y a le gaz et l'eau courante dans la cuisine; il y a même une lessiveuse.
13. — C'est parfait. Quelle sorte d'éclairage? Et puis, il y a au moins une salle de bain?
14. — Vous avez l'électricité dans toutes les chambres, une très belle salle de bain, et deux cabinets de toilette.
15. — Quel est le prix du loyer pour la saison?
16. — Pour deux mois, c'est-à-dire du 15 juillet au 15 septembre, c'est vingt mille francs.
17. — Alors je préfère rester chez moi.

LE QUATORZE JUILLET

July Fourteenth

1. — Voulez-vous me dire quelque chose de la fête du quatorze juillet?
2. — Eh bien, c'est notre fête nationale, en commémoration de la prise de la Bastille.
3. — Oui, je sais. Mais je voudrais savoir ce qu'on fait particulièrement ce jour-là.

10. Everything except linen and silverware, which you'll have to supply yourself.
11. What conveniences are there?
12. There's gas, and running water in the kitchen; there's even a washing machine.
13. That's fine. What kind of lighting? And then, is there at least one bathroom?
14. You have electricity in all the rooms, a very fine bathroom and two lavatories.

15. What is the rent for the season?
16. For two months, that is from July 15 to September 15, it's twenty thousand francs.
17. In that case I prefer to stay home.

63

1. Will you tell me something about (the) July fourteenth (holiday)?
2. Well, it's our national holiday, in commemoration of the taking of the Bastille.
3. Yes, I know. But I'd like to know what people specially do on that day.

4. — D'abord, la veille du quatorze, on passe une grande partie de la nuit à danser.

5. — On organise des bals chez des amis?
6. — Oh, non! On danse en pleine rue, et tout le monde s'amuse follement.
7. — Comment peut-on danser en pleine rue? Ça doit gêner la circulation?
8. — Pas du tout. Certaines rues sont barrées et on y dresse une estrade pour les musiciens.
9. — Et dans la journée du quatorze, qu'est-ce qui se passe d'intéressant?
10. — Il y a les grandes revues militaires, les courses de chevaux, les représentations théâtrales gratuites.
11. — Vous voulez dire qu'on peut voir une pièce de théâtre sans payer?
12. — Parfaitement. L'entrée des théâtres subventionnés est gratuite ce jour-là, et on s'y précipite en foule.
13. — Chez nous, en Amérique, les enfants aiment à tirer des pétards et à faire beaucoup de bruit le jour du quatre juillet.
14. — En France, ce sont les orateurs politiques qui font le plus grand bruit.
15. — Il n'y a pas de feu d'artifice?
16. — Oh, si. La fête du quatorze juillet se termine par un grand feu d'artifice.
17. — J'aimerais bien être en France ce jour-là.

4. First of all, on the thirteenth (lit. 'the eve of the fourteenth'), they spend a great part of the night dancing.
5. Are dances organized at the homes of friends?
6. Oh, no! People dance right in the street, and everybody has a glorious time.
7. How can they dance in the middle of the street? That must interfere with traffic?
8. Not at all. Certain streets are closed and a stand is erected for the musicians.
9. And what interesting things happen on the day of the fourteenth?
10. There are great military reviews, horse races, and free theatrical performances.

11. You mean to say that one can see a play for nothing (lit. 'without paying')?
12. Certainly. Admission to subsidized theaters is free on that day, and people flock to them.

13. At home, in America, children like to set off firecrackers and make a lot of noise on the Fourth of July.
14. In France, political speakers are the ones who make the most noise.
15. There are no fireworks?
16. Oh, yes. The fourteenth of July holiday ends with a big (display of) fireworks.
17. I should like to be in France on that day.

LA FÊTE DE NOËL (*a*)

Christmas (a)

1. — Est-ce qu'on célèbre la fête de Noël en France comme en Amérique ?
2. — A ce qu'on m'a dit, nous ne fêtons pas la Noël en France avec autant d'éclat que chez vous.
3. — Nous autres[1] Américains, nous considérons la Noël comme la plus grande fête de l'année.
4. — Chez nous la Noël est avant tout une solennité religieuse.
5. — En Amérique elle est devenue une institution commerciale de premier ordre.
6. — Mais n'est-elle pas aussi, comme en France, une occasion de réjouissance pour les membres de la famille et pour leurs amis ?
7. — Oui, sans doute. Mais pendant tout le mois de décembre les magasins font des chiffres d'affaires énormes.
8. — Qu'est-ce qu'on vend spécialement à cette occasion ?
9. — Toutes sortes de cadeaux et des quantités de cartes de Noël.
10. — En France il n'y a ni cadeaux ni cartes de Noël. Du moins, pas en général.

64

1. Is Christmas celebrated in France as in America?

2. From what I've been told, we do not celebrate Christmas in France with as much splendor as in your country.
3. We Americans consider Christmas the biggest holiday of the year.

4. With us Christmas is above all a religious celebration.
5. In America it has become a first-class commercial institution.
6. But isn't it also, as in France, an occasion for merrymaking by members of the family and their friends?
7. Yes, undoubtedly. But during the whole month of December the stores do an enormous business.
8. What is sold especially at that time?

9. All kinds of gifts and quantities of Christmas cards.
10. In France there are neither gifts nor Christmas cards. At least not generally.

11. — Mais vous avez des arbres de Noël comme en Amérique?
12. — Dans certaines familles, oui. Mais cette coutume n'est pas très répandue en France.
13. — Et les enfants, est-ce qu'ils ne reçoivent pas des cadeaux de Noël?
14. — Si, mais modérément. On leur offre quelques jouets, des poupées, des bonbons.

[1] **autres** is sometimes used with **nous** and **vous** for emphasis.

LA FÊTE DE NOËL (*b*)

Christmas (*b*)

1. — Mais, dites-moi donc, en France on ne fait rien de spécial pour la fête de Noël?
2. — Ah, si. Nous avons le réveillon.
3. — Qu'est-ce que c'est que le réveillon?
4. — Eh bien, c'est un souper qu'on sert dans la nuit de Noël.
5. — Et en quoi consiste ce souper?
6. — Des huîtres sont de rigueur, puis une oie rôtie, puis un gâteau spécial, et naturellement du champagne.

11. But don't you have Christmas trees as in America?
12. In certain families, yes. But that custom is not very widespread in France.
13. And don't the children receive Christmas presents?
14. Yes, but in moderation. They are given a few toys, dolls, and some candy.

65

1. But tell me, don't they do anything special in France for Christmas?
2. Oh, yes. We have the *réveillon.*
3. What is the *réveillon?*
4. Well, it's a supper that's served on Christmas Eve.
5. And what does that supper consist of?
6. Oysters are obligatory, then a roast goose, then a special cake, and naturally champagne.

7. — Vous me disiez que ce n'est pas l'habitude de s'adresser des cartes de Noël.
8. — En effet. C'est plutôt l'exception.
9. — Cependant, en Amérique, on trouve des cartes de Noël qui sont en français.
10. — C'est vrai, mais c'est pour les Américains ou pour les Français d'Amérique.
11. — Mais est-ce qu'on ne se souhaite pas un « *Happy Christmas* »?
12. — Non. Cela n'est pas non plus une coutume française. Cependant, si on envoie une carte de Noël à quelqu'un, on y met d'habitude: Joyeux Noël!
13. — Je m'étonne qu'on ne se fasse [1] pas des cadeaux comme chez nous.
14. — Il n'y a pas de quoi s'étonner. D'après ce qu'on m'a dit, en Amérique les cadeaux de Noël sont une obligation sociale plutôt qu'un plaisir.
15. — C'est vrai. Vous n'avez pas idée de la peine qu'on se donne pour se faire des douzaines de cadeaux.
16. — Et à qui donc offre-t-on tout cela?
17. — Aux parents, aux amis, aux domestiques, aux patrons, aux employés, à toutes sortes de gens à tort et à travers.
18. — C'est un peu comme cela chez nous pour le Jour de l'An.

[1] § 27*a*.

7. You were telling me that it isn't customary to send Christmas cards.
8. That's right. It is rather the exception.
9. However, in America one finds Christmas cards which are in French.
10. That's true, but they are for Americans or for French people in America.
11. But don't people wish one another a "Happy Christmas"?
12. No. That's not a French custom either. Nevertheless, if you send a Christmas card to anyone, you generally write: *Joyeux Noël!*

13. I'm surprised that you don't exchange gifts as we do.
14. There's nothing to be surprised about. According to what I've been told, Christmas gifts in America are a social obligation rather than a pleasure.
15. That's true. You have no idea how troublesome it is to exchange dozens of gifts.

16. And to whom are they all given?
17. To relatives, friends, servants, employers, employees, to all kinds of people without rhyme or reason.
18. It's a little like that with us on New Year's Day.

LE NOUVEL AN

New Year's

1. — Pour les Français la fête du Jour de l'An est plus importante que la Noël, n'est-ce pas?
2. — C'est que le Jour de l'An est une fête bien différente de celle de Noël.
3. — En quoi donc ces deux fêtes diffèrent-elles principalement?
4. — Eh bien, comme je vous le disais, la Noël est avant tout une fête religieuse. Mais le Jour de l'An est uniquement une fête mondaine.
5. — Que voulez-vous dire par une fête mondaine?
6. — C'est qu'à cette occasion on observe certaines coutumes sociales. Par exemple, on fait de nombreuses visites.
7. — Est-ce qu'on souhaite une bonne année comme chez nous en Amérique?
8. — Assurément. On dit: « Je vous souhaite une bonne année », ou simplement « Bonne Année! »
9. — Mais y a-t-il une façon spéciale de célébrer cette fête?
10. — C'est surtout la veille du premier de l'An qui est une occasion de réjouissances.
11. — Est-ce qu'au coup de minuit on fait un grand vacarme comme chez nous en Amérique?

66

1. For the French, New Year's Day is more important than Christmas, isn't it?
2. The fact is that New Year's Day is a holiday quite different from Christmas.
3. In what respect do those two holidays differ principally?
4. Well, as I was telling you, Christmas is above all a religious celebration. But New Year's is purely a social holiday.
5. What do you mean by a social holiday?
6. On that occasion certain social customs are observed. For instance, one makes many calls.

7. Do you wish one another a happy New Year as we do in America?
8. Certainly. One says: "I wish you a good year," or simply "Good Year!"

9. But is there a special manner of celebrating that holiday?
10. New Year's Eve is above all an occasion for merrymaking.
11. Do you make a lot of racket at the stroke of twelve as we do in America?

12. — Mais non. La veille du Nouvel An on va au bal ou bien au théâtre, puis vers minuit, comme à Noël, il y a un réveillon.
13. — Vous me disiez qu'on faisait des cadeaux à l'occasion du Premier de l'An.
14. — En effet; entre parents et amis intimes on s'offre des étrennes, mais avec la plus grande réserve. On donne aussi quelque rémunération aux gens de service de la maison.

LA BRETAGNE

Brittany

1. — On m'a conseillé de faire un tour en Bretagne cet été. Connaissez-vous cette province?
2. — Mais oui, très bien. J'y ai passé plusieurs étés bien agréables.
3. — Qu'est-ce qu'il y a de particulièrement intéressant en cette région?
4. — Le paysage, les gens, les coutumes, tout y est différent du reste de la France.
5. — Je n'ai jamais compris pourquoi ce pays s'appelle la Bretagne. Est-ce que vous le savez?

12. Oh, no. On New Year's Eve we go to a ball or to the theater; then about midnight, as at Christmas, there is a *réveillon* (midnight supper).
13. You told me that you gave presents on New Year's Day.
14. So we do; among relatives and intimate friends, New Year's gifts are exchanged, but in great moderation. One also gives a little bonus to the employees in one's household.

67

1. I was advised to take a trip to Brittany this summer. Do you know that province?
2. Oh yes, very well. I have spent several very pleasant summers there.
3. What is there of special interest in that region?
4. The scenery, the people, the customs, everything there is different from the rest of France.
5. I have never understood why that country is called Brittany. Do you know?

6. — C'est parce que les Bretons sont originaires de la Grande Bretagne.
7. — Vraiment? Je ne savais pas ça. Quand donc ont-ils quitté leur pays d'origine?
8. — A l'époque des invasions anglo-saxonnes, c'est-à-dire vers le cinquième siècle.
9. — Mais alors, les Bretons sont de race celtique?
10. — Oui, comme les Irlandais ou les Gallois.
11. — Quelle langue parlent-ils?
12. — Une langue spéciale qu'on appelle le breton.
13. — A quoi ressemble cette langue?
14. — Elle ressemble beaucoup au gallois.
15. — Alors, les Bretons ne parlent pas français?
16. — Mais si, ils parlent les deux langues.
17. — On m'a parlé aussi des pardons de Bretagne, mais je ne sais pas exactement ce que c'est.

18. — Un pardon est une sorte de pèlerinage à la chapelle d'un saint local, et c'est aussi l'occasion de réjouissances populaires.
19. — Est-ce que les Bretons portent encore leurs costumes pittoresques?
20. — Oui, surtout les gens de la campagne. Les femmes, en particulier, portent toujours leurs jolies coiffes et leurs tabliers brodés.
21. — Ça doit être un pays bien intéressant. Il faut que j'aille y faire un tour cet été.

6. Because the Bretons originally came from Great Britain.
7. Really? I didn't know that. But when did they leave their original country?
8. At the time of the Anglo-Saxon invasions, that is, about the fifth century.
9. Then the Bretons are Celtic (lit. 'of Celtic race')?
10. Yes, like the Irish or the Welsh.
11. What language do they speak?
12. A special language called Breton.
13. What language does it resemble?
14. It resembles Welsh a great deal.
15. Then the Bretons do not speak French?
16. Oh yes, they speak both languages.
17. I was also told about the *pardons* (pilgrimages) in Brittany, but I don't exactly know what they are.
18. A *pardon* is a sort of pilgrimage to the chapel of some local saint, and it is also an occasion for popular merrymaking.
19. Do the Bretons still wear their picturesque costumes?
20. Yes, especially the country folk. The women, in particular, always wear their pretty headdresses and their embroidered aprons.
21. It must be a very interesting country. I'll have to take a trip there this summer.

A TRAVERS LA FRANCE

Through France

1. — Quelles sont les autres régions de la France que je devrais visiter?
2. — Écoutez: puisque vous comptez aller en Bretagne, passez donc par la Touraine.
3. — C'est là que se trouvent ces beaux châteaux, n'est-ce pas?
4. — Mais oui, les châteaux de la Loire. Et puis, après avoir visité la Bretagne, vous pourriez revenir par la Normandie.
5. — Ça, c'est une bonne idée. Oui, il faut absolument que je fasse un tour en Normandie.
6. — Vous avez raison. Vous aimerez les belles plages de la côte normande, Trouville, par exemple.
7. — Oui, il y a beaucoup à voir en France en été. Mais en hiver, où pourrait-on aller?
8. — Aimez-vous les sports d'hiver?
9. — Je n'en raffole pas. Cependant j'aime assez le ski.
10. — Dans ce cas, vous devriez passer quelques semaines à Chamonix.
11. — Chamonix? C'est dans les Alpes, ça, n'est-ce pas?
12. — Oui, c'est une station d'hiver très fréquentée.

68

1. What other regions of France should I visit?

2. Look here: since you plan to go to Brittany, then go through Touraine.
3. That's where all those beautiful châteaux are, isn't it?
4. Yes, the châteaux of the Loire. And then, after visiting Brittany, you could return through Normandy.
5. That's a good idea. Yes, I absolutely must take a trip to Normandy.
6. You're right. You'll like the fine beaches along the Normandy coast, Trouville for instance.

7. Yes, there's a great deal to see in France in the summer. But where could I go in winter?
8. Do you like winter sports?
9. I'm not crazy about them. However, I like skiing well enough.
10. In that case, you ought to spend a few weeks at Chamonix.
11. Chamonix? That's in the Alps, isn't it?

12. Yes, it's a great winter resort. But naturally

Mais naturellement il faudra que vous alliez aussi sur la Côte d'Azur.

13. — J'espère que oui. Le climat du midi doit être bien agréable.

14. — Très agréable. Que ce soit à Cannes, à Nice ou à Menton, il fait un temps très doux, et le paysage est de toute beauté.

VOYAGE EN AVION

An Airplane Trip

1. — J'ai l'intention de faire un voyage au Maroc au printemps prochain. Y êtes-vous jamais allé?
2. — Mais oui, j'y suis allé le mois dernier en avion.
3. — Tiens! moi aussi, je compte prendre la route des airs. Et vous avez fait un bon voyage?
4. — Superbe. Et c'est si pratique. Pensez donc! En cinq heures de temps on arrive à Rabat.
5. — Vous ne vous êtes pas senti mal à cause de l'altitude?
6. — Mais non. D'ailleurs on ne vole pas bien haut, sauf au-dessus des Pyrénées.

you'll also have to go to the Riviera (*or* the Côte d'Azur).

13. I hope so. The southern climate must be very pleasant.
14. Very pleasant. Whether (it be) at Cannes, Nice, or Menton, the climate is very mild, and the scenery is extremely beautiful.

69

1. I intend to take a trip to Morocco next spring. Have you ever gone there?
2. Oh yes, I went there last month by plane.
3. Well! I too plan to take the air route. And did you have a nice trip?
4. First-rate. And it's so practical. Just think! In five hours' time you reach Rabat.
5. Didn't you feel sick because of the altitude?
6. Oh, no. Anyway they don't fly very high, except over the Pyrenees.

7. — Moi, ça me fait toujours mal aux oreilles quand on dépasse trois mille mètres.
8. — Moi, pas du tout. L'altitude ne me gêne pas.
9. — Vous n'avez pas eu de tempête?
10. — Non, le vol a été très calme, sauf au-dessus des Pyrénées, où il y avait quelques « poches d'air ».
11. — La compagnie fournit le transport à l'aérodrome, n'est-ce pas?
12. — Tout est fourni. Au départ on vient vous chercher à domicile, et à l'arrivée on vous dépose à votre hôtel.
13. — A combien de bagages a-t-on droit?
14. — A une quinzaine de kilos, je crois.
15. — Vous avez sans doute pris l'avion à l'aéroport du Bourget.
16. — Oui, c'est tout près de Paris.
17. — Vous n'avez pas fait escale?
18. — Si, on a fait escale à Bordeaux, et après ça on a filé tout droit vers le Maroc.
19. — Ainsi vous avez survolé les Pyrénées et la Méditerranée?
20. — C'est ça. Et nous avons atterri à Rabat sans le moindre incident.

Additional Vocabulary: **une aile,** *wing;* **décoller,** *to take off;* **amérir,** *to come down* (on water); **un avion de bombardement,** *bombing plane;* **un avion de chasse,** *pursuit plane;* **le hangar,**

7. My ears always ache when I go beyond three thousand meters.
8. Mine never do. The altitude doesn't bother me.
9. Didn't you have any storm?
10. No, the flight was very calm, except above the Pyrenees, where there were some air pockets.

11. The company furnishes transportation to the airfield, doesn't it?
12. Everything is furnished. When you leave they call for you at your home, and when you arrive they take you to your hotel.
13. How much baggage is one allowed?
14. About fifteen kilos, I think.
15. No doubt you took the plane at Le Bourget airport.
16. Yes, it is very close to Paris.
17. You didn't make any stop?
18. Yes, we stopped at Bordeaux, and after that we flew straight to Morocco.
19. Then you flew over the Pyrenees and the Mediterranean?
20. That's right. And we landed at Rabat without the slightest mishap.

hangar; **le mécanicien,** *mechanic;* **le moteur,** *motor;* **le parachute,** *parachute;* **le pilote,** *pilot;* **j'ai fait une partie du trajet en avion,** *I flew part of the way.*

LE COMMIS VOYAGEUR

The Traveling Salesman

1. — J'aimerais parler au gérant, s.v.p.
2. — C'est moi le gérant. A qui ai-je l'honneur de parler ?
3. — Je suis le représentant de la maison Machin, frères. Je voudrais vous montrer quelques échantillons de nos articles (produits).
4. — Votre maison nous est connue, monsieur. Nous sommes très satisfaits de votre dernier envoi.
5. — En ce cas, je suis persuadé que vous trouverez ce qui vous convient parmi nos dernières nouveautés.
6. — Ces dessins me plaisent beaucoup. Cette étoffe m'intéresse aussi. Combien se vend-elle ?
7. — Nous vous ferons un prix spécial, et nous vous l'expédierons franco de port.
8. — Quelles sont les conditions de payement ?
9. — Les payements se font dans six mois, à dater de la facture. Rabais de cinq pour cent au comptant.
10. — Le payement dans six mois me convient. Quels sont les droits à payer sur cet article ?
11. — Dix pour cent seulement.

1. I should like to speak with the manager, please.
2. I'm the manager. (Whom have I the honor of addressing?)
3. I'm the representative of Machin Brothers. I should like to show you some samples of our merchandise (products).
4. We know your firm. We are very much satisfied with your last shipment.

5. In that case I'm sure you will find something that will suit you among our latest novelties.

6. I like these designs very much. I'm interested in this material, too. What does it sell for?

7. We'll make a special price to you, and we'll send it prepaid.
8. What are the terms?
9. Payment in six months from date of invoice. Five per cent discount for cash.

10. Payment in six months suits me. What is the duty on this article?
11. Only ten per cent.

12. — C'est bien. Pourriez-vous m'en faire la livraison dans deux semaines?
13. — Soyez sans crainte. Votre commande sera exécutée [1] en tous points selon vos désirs.
14. — C'est donc convenu. Au revoir, monsieur, et bonne chance!

[1] **vos ordres seront exécutés,** *your wishes will be carried out.*

Additional Vocabulary: **une agence de publicité,** *advertising agency;* **faire de la réclame (de la publicité),** *to advertise;* **le panneau réclame,** *advertising sign (panel).*

LA DACTYLOGRAPHE

The Typist

1. — Mademoiselle, vous m'avez été recommandée comme dactylo. Etes-vous libre ce matin?
2. — Oui, monsieur, je suis à votre service.
3. — J'ai plusieurs lettres à dicter. Et puis une circulaire que je voudrais faire taper à plusieurs exemplaires.
4. — Je suis à votre disposition pour faire tous les travaux de cette sorte.
5. — Quels sont vos prix, mademoiselle?
6. — D'habitude je fais payer trois francs la page, et trois francs soixante-quinze pour trois exemplaires.

12. All right. Could you deliver it to me in two weeks?
13. Don't worry. Your order will be filled exactly as you wish.
14. That's settled then. Good-bye, sir, and good luck!

expédition (envoi)	**par express**	*sent by express*
	par petite vitesse	*by freight*
	par avion	*by plane*
payement contre livraison		*C.O.D.*

71

1. (Miss), you were recommended to me as a typist. Are you free this morning?
2. Yes, sir, at your service.
3. I have several letters to dictate. And a circular of which I should like to have several copies typed.
4. I'm ready to do all jobs of that kind.

5. What are your rates, (Miss)?
6. Generally I ask three francs a page, and three francs seventy-five (centimes) for three copies.

7. — Je puis compter sur un travail soigné, n'est-ce pas?
8. — Oh, monsieur, je vous garantis un travail impeccable pour tout ce que je tape à la machine.
9. — Vous savez sans doute aussi la sténographie?
10. — Oui, monsieur; je suis sténodactylo et je peux prendre des dictées même très rapides.
11. — Pour ma lettre circulaire, je voudrais en faire tirer deux cents exemplaires au duplicateur (multigraphe).[1] Savez-vous vous servir de cet appareil?
12. — Mais oui, monsieur; j'en ai l'habitude et je me charge de vous tirer autant d'exemplaires que vous voudrez.
13. — Bien, mademoiselle. Je vais d'abord vous dicter une lettre d'affaires. Etes-vous prête?
14. — Oui, monsieur. Vous pouvez commencer.

[1] **un double au carbone,** *carbon copy;* **le papier carbone,** *carbon paper;* **un exemplaire en triple (quadruple) au papier carbone,** *three (four) carbon copies;* **le ruban à encre,** (*inked*) *ribbon;* **écrit à la**

POUR SOLLICITER UNE PLACE

Applying for a Position

1. — Bonjour, mademoiselle. Vous venez solliciter une place de secrétaire?

7. I can depend on careful work, can't I?

8. Oh (sir), I guarantee faultless work in all my typing.
9. No doubt you also know shorthand?
10. Yes, sir; I'm a shorthand-typist and I can take very rapid dictation.
11. For my circular letter, I'd like to have two hundred copies mimeographed. Do you know how to use that machine?

12. Yes, sir; I'm used to it, and I can make as many copies as you wish.

13. Very well, (Miss). First I'll dictate a business letter. Are you ready?
14. Yes, sir. You may begin.

machine, *typewritten;* **le papier pour machine à écrire,** *typewriter paper;* **le caractère,** *type;* **la touche,** *key.*

72

1. Good morning, (Miss). Have you come to apply for a position as secretary?

2. — Oui, monsieur. J'ai lu votre annonce dans le journal du matin.
3. — Nous cherchons quelqu'un qui puisse se charger de la correspondance étrangère.
4. — Je crois pouvoir remplir les conditions exigées.
5. — Quelles langues savez-vous à fond?
6. — Je parle et j'écris couramment le français, l'anglais et l'espagnol.
7. — Comment vous êtes-vous préparée aux fonctions de secrétaire?
8. — J'ai suivi les cours de l'École de Commerce de Chicago.
9. — Vous avez déjà été engagée dans quelque maison d'importance?
10. — J'ai travaillé trois ans chez Messieurs Marchand et Cie à New York.
11. — Nous sommes en rapport avec cette maison. Vous avez sans doute des certificats?
12. — Oui, monsieur. Je puis vous en laisser les copies, si vous désirez les examiner.
13. — Oui, laissez-les-moi, je vous prie, mademoiselle. Elles me permettront de juger de vos aptitudes.
14. — J'espère, monsieur, que vous accueillerez favorablement ma demande.
15. — Vous voudrez bien repasser dans deux jours. Bonjour, mademoiselle.
16. — Bonjour, monsieur.

2. Yes, sir. I read your advertisement in this morning's paper.
3. We are looking for someone who can take care of the foreign correspondence.
4. I think I can fulfill the requirements.
5. What languages do you know thoroughly?
6. I speak and write French, English, and Spanish fluently.
7. What was your training for the job of secretary?
8. I took the Chicago School of Commerce courses.
9. Have you already worked for a large firm?
10. I worked three years at Marchand & Company in New York.
11. We have connections with that firm. You no doubt have references?
12. Yes, sir. I can leave copies with you if you wish to look them over.
13. Yes, leave them with me, please, (Miss). They will enable me to judge your qualifications.
14. I hope (sir) that you will act favorably on my application.
15. Will you please come back in two days. Good-bye, (Miss).
16. Good-bye, sir.

FORMULES DE CORRESPONDANCE

Forms of Letters

I. En s'adressant à un homme:

A. *En-tête.* — L'en-tête varie selon le degré des relations sociales entre correspondants.

1. Monsieur; Cher Monsieur; Cher Monsieur et ami; Cher ami. On ne dit jamais: Mon cher Monsieur. Il faut aussi éviter de dire: Cher Monsieur Dupont, etc.
2. Monsieur; Mon cher Docteur (Maître pour avocats); Cher Docteur (Maître) et ami; Mon cher Confrère (entre docteurs et avocats).
3. Monsieur le Président (le Ministre, le Sénateur, le Directeur, etc.)

B. *Formules finales.* — On répète toujours, dans la formule finale, les mêmes mots qui ont servi pour l'en-tête.

Voici les formules les plus habituelles dans l'ordre du degré des relations sociales entre correspondants.

1. Je vous prie d'agréer, Monsieur, l'expression de mes sentiments respectueux.
2. Recevez, Monsieur, l'assurance de ma considération la plus distinguée (de mes sentiments les plus distingués).

73

I. Addressing a man:

A. *Heading.* — The heading varies according to the degree of social relationship between correspondents.

1. Sir; Dear Sir; Dear Sir and Friend; Dear Friend. One never says: My dear Sir. One must also avoid saying: Dear Mr. Dupont, etc.

2. Sir; My dear Doctor (*Maître* for lawyers); Dear Doctor (*Maître*) and Friend; My dear Colleague (among doctors and lawyers).
3. Mr. President (Minister, Senator, Director, etc.).

B. *Endings.* — The same words that have been used in the heading are always repeated in the ending.

The most usual forms in the order of the degree of social relationship between correspondents are these:

1. Yours respectfully (lit. 'I beg you to accept, Sir, the expression of my respectful sentiments').
2. Sincerely yours, Very truly yours (lit. 'Receive, Sir, the assurance of . . .').

3. Recevez, cher Monsieur, l'assurance de mes meilleurs sentiments (de mes sentiments très cordiaux).
4. Recevez, cher ami, l'assurance de ma plus cordiale sympathie.
5. Dans une lettre intime et familière on peut terminer à l'américaine: Cordialement vôtre; Bien sincèrement à vous, etc.

II. En s'adressant à une femme:

A. *En-tête.*

Madame; Chère Madame; Chère Madame et amie; Chère amie.
On ne dit jamais: Chère Madame Dupont, etc.

B. *Formules finales.*

1. Je vous prie d'agréer, . . ., mes hommages les plus respectueux.
2. Je vous prie d'agréer, . . ., avec mes hommages l'expression de ma plus respectueuse sympathie.

A un degré plus intime, le cœur dictera la formule.

Correspondance commerciale

A. *Commande de marchandises.*

Lyon, le 10 janvier 19—
Messieurs Lenoir, Leblanc et Cie

Messieurs,

Je vous prie de m'expédier le plus tôt possible par express les articles suivants: . . .

3. Very sincerely yours (lit. 'Receive, dear Sir, the assurance of . . . ').

4. Cordially yours (lit. 'Receive, dear friend, the assurance . . .').

5. In a familiar and intimate letter one can end in the American fashion: Cordially yours; Yours sincerely, etc.

II. Addressing a woman:

A. *Heading.*

Madam; Dear Madam; Dear Madam and Friend; Dear Friend.

One never says: Dear Madam Dupont, etc.

B. *Endings.*

1. Yours respectfully (lit. 'I beg you to accept, etc.').

2. Sincerely yours (lit. 'I beg you to accept, etc.').

In a more intimate degree, the heart will dictate the form.

Commercial Correspondence

A. *An order for merchandise.*

Lyons, January 10, 19—

Lenoir, Leblanc & Co.

Gentlemen:

Please send me the following articles as soon as possible by express: . . .

Comme j'ai un besoin pressant de ces marchandises, ayez l'obligeance de me faire savoir par retour du courrier si je puis compter les recevoir avant la fin du mois.

S'il vous est impossible de les livrer avant le 28 courant, vous voudrez bien considérer mon ordre comme nul et non avenu.

Veuillez agréer, Messieurs, l'expression de mes sentiments distingués.

B. *Réponse à la lettre précédente.*

Monsieur,

Conformément à votre demande du 10 courant, nous avons l'honneur de vous informer que votre ordre sera exécuté dans le plus bref délai. Selon vos désirs les marchandises faisant l'objet de votre commande seront expédiées à votre charge par service rapide Lyon-Paris.

Nous vous prions d'agréer, Monsieur, nos salutations empressées.

Une Invitation

Le Colonel et Madame de Beaupré prient Monsieur et Madame Richardson de leur faire l'honneur de venir dîner chez eux le samedi quinze mars prochain à huit heures et demie.

Réponse à l'invitation précédente

A. *Acceptation.*

Monsieur et Madame Paul V. Richardson présentent leurs meilleurs compliments au Colonel et

As I am in urgent need of this merchandise, will you please let me know by return mail whether I can count on receiving it before the end of the month.

If it is impossible for you to deliver it before the 28th of this month, will you please consider my order as cancelled.

Very truly yours,

B. *Reply to the preceding letter.*

Dear Sir,

Complying with your request of the 10th of this month, we are glad (lit. 'honored') to inform you that your order will be filled as soon as possible. In accordance with your wishes the merchandise you ordered will be sent at your expense by the Lyons-Paris express.

Yours truly,

An Invitation

Colonel and Mrs. de Beaupré request the honor of Mr. and Mrs. Richardson's company at dinner on next Saturday, March fifteenth, at half past eight o'clock.

Reply to the Preceding Invitation

A. *Accepting.*

Mr. and Mrs. Paul V. Richardson present their compliments to Colonel and Mrs. de Beaupré and

à Madame de Beaupré et les remercient de leur aimable invitation à laquelle ils seront très heureux de se rendre.

B. *Refus.*

Monsieur et Madame Paul V. Richardson prient le Colonel et Madame de Beaupré d'agréer l'assurance de leur respectueuse sympathie et les remercient de leur invitation à laquelle ils auront le regret de ne pouvoir se rendre, étant retenus par des engagements antérieurs.

Souhaits de fête

Permettez-moi de vous offrir, à l'occasion de votre fête, mes meilleurs souhaits (mes vœux les plus sympathiques; mes souhaits les plus cordiaux; mes souhaits affectueux, etc.).

Entre intimes, on pourra dire tout simplement: « Bonne et heureuse fête! »

thank them for their kind invitation, which they are happy to accept.

B. *Declining.*

Mr. and Mrs. Paul V. Richardson present their compliments to Colonel and Mrs. de Beaupré and thank them for their invitation, which they regret not being able to accept because of previous engagements.

Birthday (*or* Name-Day) Greetings

Many happy returns of the day, etc.

Among intimate friends one can simply say: "Happy birthday!"

APPENDIX

APPENDIX

1. Gender

Nouns are either masculine or feminine. Nouns denoting male beings are masculine. Nouns denoting female beings are feminine. The gender of other nouns must be learned by usage.

2. The Definite Article *the*

	SINGULAR		PLURAL	
Masc.	**le**		**les**	
Fem.	**la**		**les**	
le timbre	the stamp		**les timbres**	the stamps
l'avion	the plane		**les avions**	the planes
la cigarette	the cigarette		**les cigarettes**	the cigarettes
l'heure	the hour		**les heures**	the hours

Le and **la** become **l'** before a vowel or mute **h.**

Contraction

de + le = du of (from) the　　**à + le = au** to (at, in) the
de + les = des of (from) the　　**à + les = aux** to (at, in) the
de + la and **de + l'**, **à + la** and **à + l'** do not contract.

le plan du bateau
the plan of the boat
la visite des passeports
the passport inspection

Je vais au cinéma.
I am going to the "movies."
Il parle aux employés.
He speaks to the employees.

The definite article is used

a) With nouns denoting all of a class:

Les femmes aiment les bijoux. Women like jewels.

b) With abstract nouns:

Le courage est nécessaire.	Courage is necessary.

c) With adjectives denoting a language:

L'anglais est difficile.	English is difficult.

Except after **parler** and **en:**

Il parle français et je traduis en anglais.	He speaks French and I translate into English.

d) With geographical names (**la France, l'Angleterre, le Canada, l'Amérique,** etc.) except after **en:**

La France est un beau pays.	France is a beautiful country.
Il va au Canada.	He is going to Canada.
Je vais en France.	I am going to France.

Geographical names ending in silent **e** are usually feminine; others are masculine. Exception: **le Mexique,** *Mexico.*

e) With a title not in direct address, except with **monsieur, madame, mademoiselle:**

Le général Leblanc est ici.	General White is here.
Monsieur Lenoir est à Paris.	Mr. Black is in Paris.

f) With nouns of weight and measure:

Cela coûte vingt francs le mètre.	That costs twenty francs a meter.

g) Instead of possessive adjectives with parts of the body:

Que tenez-vous à la main?	What are you holding in your hand?

h) With names of seasons, expressions of time, meals, etc.:

Le printemps est arrivé.	Spring has come.
Le dîner est à huit heures.	Dinner is at eight.

i) With **de** to indicate a partitive noun:

Avez-vous du pain?	Have you (some) bread?
J'ai de l'argent.	I have (some) money.
J'ai de l'encre.	I have (some) ink.
Il a des timbres.	He has (some) stamps.

Except: 1) in a negation; 2) when an adjective precedes the noun; 3) after an expression of quantity:

Je n'ai pas de timbres.	I have no stamps.
Elle a de grands yeux.	She has big eyes.
J'ai assez d'argent.	I have enough money.

3. The Indefinite Article *a, an*

	SINGULAR		PLURAL	
Masc.	**un**	a (one)	**des**	some
Fem.	**une**	a (one)	**des**	some

Donnez-moi un timbre.	Give me a stamp.
Donnez-moi des timbres.	Give me some stamps.

4. The indefinite article is omitted

a) Before unmodified nouns indicating nationality or profession:

Je suis Français.	I am a Frenchman.
Il est aviateur.	He is an aviator.

b) Before **cent** and **mille:**

J'ai cent (mille) francs.	I have a hundred (a thousand) francs.

5. Plural of Nouns

a) Nouns regularly form their plural by adding **s** to the singular. If the singular ends in **s**, there is no change.

le timbre	the stamp	**les timbres**	the stamps
le fils	the son	**les fils**	the sons

b) Nouns ending in **au** or **eu** take **x** instead of **s**, and names ending in **al** change to **aux:**

le chapeau	the hat	**les chapeaux**	the hats
le cheval	the horse	**les chevaux**	the horses

6. Adjectives agree in gender and number with the nouns they modify.

a) The feminine of most adjectives is formed by adding **e** to the masculine:

un grand pays	a large country
une grande ville	a large city

b) Adjectives ending in **e** are invariable in the singular:

un homme riche	a rich man
une femme riche	a rich woman

c) There are some exceptional feminine endings, such as:

bon, bonne	good	**beau, belle**	beautiful
blanc, blanche	white	**doux, douce**	sweet

7. Position of Adjectives

Adjectives may precede or follow the noun. A few generally precede: **petit, grand, beau,** etc.

A few generally follow: adjectives of nationality and of color:

une petite maison	a little house
une robe bleue	a blue gown
un livre français	a French book

8. Comparison

Place **plus,** *more*, **moins,** *less*, **aussi,** *as*, **si,** *so*, before the adjective or adverb; and **que,** *than*, *as*, after it:

Pierre est plus grand que Paul.	Peter is taller than Paul.
Paul parle moins bien que Pierre.	Paul speaks less well than Peter.

Henri est aussi grand qu'Albert.	Henry is as tall as Albert.
Georges n'est pas si grand que vous.	George is not so tall as you.

In the superlative, place the definite article or possessive adjective before **plus** or **moins:**

le plus beau jardin	the most beautiful garden
la plus grande maison	the largest house
le plus souvent	most often

Irregular Comparisons

bon	good	**meilleur**	better	**le meilleur**	the best
bien	well	**mieux**	better	**le mieux**	the best
peu	little	**moins**	less	**le moins**	the least

9. Possessive Adjectives

	SINGULAR		PLURAL
	Masc.	*Fem.*	*Masc. and Fem.*
my	**mon**	**ma**	**mes**
thy	**ton**	**ta**	**tes**
his / her / its	**son**	**sa**	**ses**
our	**notre**	**notre**	**nos**
your	**votre**	**votre**	**vos**
their	**leur**	**leur**	**leurs**

10. The possessive adjective agrees with the noun that comes immediately after it, and it must be repeated before each noun:

mon père et ma mère	my father and mother
Victor et sa sœur	Victor and his sister
Hélène et son frère	Helen and her brother
vos parents et leurs enfants	your parents and their children

Mon, ton, son are used instead of **ma, ta, sa** before feminine singular nouns beginning with a vowel or mute **h:**

mon amie my lady friend

11. Possessive Pronouns

	SINGULAR		PLURAL	
	Masc.	*Fem.*	*Masc.*	*Fem.*
mine	**le mien**	**la mienne**	**les miens**	**les miennes**
yours (thine)	**le tien**	**la tienne**	**les tiens**	**les tiennes**
his / hers / its	**le sien**	**la sienne**	**les siens**	**les siennes**
ours	**le nôtre**	**la nôtre**	**les nôtres**	
yours	**le vôtre**	**la vôtre**	**les vôtres**	
theirs	**le leur**	**la leur**	**les leurs**	

12. The possessive pronouns, like possessive adjectives, agree in gender and number with the object possessed:

votre chambre et la mienne	your room and mine
mon hôtel et le sien	my hotel and his

13. Distinction of ownership is expressed by the use of the possessive pronoun. Mere ownership is expressed by **être** + **à:**

A qui sont ces mouchoirs?	Whose handkerchiefs are these?
Ils ne sont pas à moi.	They are not mine.
Les miens sont bleus.	Mine are blue.

14. Demonstrative Adjectives

this or *that* = **ce** before a masculine noun beginning with a consonant
cet before a masculine noun beginning with a vowel or a mute **h**
cette before a feminine noun
these or *those* = **ces** before any plural noun

There is no special word in French to distinguish between *this* and *that*, nor between *these* and *those*. When such distinction is necessary, **-ci,** *here*, or **-là,** *there*, is added to the noun:

Cet homme-ci est plus riche que cet homme-là.	This man is wealthier than that man.

15. Demonstrative Pronouns

Masc. Sing.	**celui**	this, that, the one
Fem. Sing.	**celle**	
Masc. Pl.	**ceux**	these, those, the ones
Fem. Pl.	**celles**	

When the demonstrative pronoun is not followed by a relative pronoun or by an adjective phrase, **-ci** or **-là** must be affixed:

Regardez ces deux tableaux.	Look at those two pictures.
Celui-ci est plus beau que celui-là.	This one is more beautiful than that one.
Voici celui que je préfère.	Here is the one I prefer.

16. Adverbs are usually formed by adding **–ment** to the feminine singular of the adjective:

parfait, –e perfect **parfaitement** perfectly

EXCEPTIONS: **bien** well **mal** badly **vite** quickly

17. Negatives

ne . . . pas	not	**ne . . . que**	only
ne . . . rien	nothing	**ne . . . plus**	no more (longer)
ne . . . jamais	never	**ne . . . personne**	nobody

a) The verb comes between **ne** and the negative word:

Je comprends. I understand.
Je ne comprends pas. I do not understand.

b) If the negative word is subject of the verb, it precedes **ne:**

Personne ne comprend. Nobody understands.

18. Personal Pronouns

SUBJECT	DIRECT OBJECT	INDIRECT OBJECT	REFLEXIVE	DISJUNCTIVE
je I	**me** me	**me** (to) me	**me** myself	**moi** me (I)
tu you (*fam.*)	**te** you	**te** (to) you	**te** yourself	**toi** you
il he, it	**le** him, it	**lui** to him	**se** himself	**lui** him (he), it
elle she, it	**la** her, it	**lui** to her	**se** herself	**elle** her (she), it
		lui to it	**se** itself	
nous we	**nous** us	**nous** (to) us	**nous** ourselves	**nous** us
vous you	**vous** you	**vous** (to) you	**vous** yourselves	**vous** you
ils they	**les** them	**leur** (to) them	**se** themselves	**eux** them
elles they				**elles** them

19. Position of Personal Pronouns

a) Object pronouns are placed before the verb:

Je le vois.	I see him.
Je ne le vois pas.	I do not see him.

b) Object pronouns follow affirmative commands but precede negative commands:

Donnez-le-moi.	Give it to me.
Ne me le donnez pas.	Don't give it to me.

c) When there are two object pronouns, the indirect precedes the direct, except when both are in the third person:

Il me le donne.	He gives it to me.
Je le lui donne.	I give it to him (her).

20. The pronoun **en** is used in reference to things

a) To replace a noun or a clause preceded by **de:**

Il aime son pays. Il en parle souvent.	He loves his country. He speaks of it often.

b) To replace a partitive:

Combien de timbres avez-vous? J'en ai deux.	How many stamps have you? I have two (of them).

21. The pronoun and adverb **y** refers to things or places preceded by **à, dans, sur, chez,** etc.

il y a there is, there are
Je vais à Paris. J'y vais. (I am going there.)
Il va chez sa mère. Il y va. (He is going there.)

22. The disjunctive forms are used

a) When the personal pronoun stands alone:

Qui est là? —Moi. Who is there? I.

b) After a preposition:

Je vais avec eux. I am going with them.

23. Interrogation

a) The words **est-ce que** may always be used to introduce a question without changing the word order:

Est-ce que vous parlez français? Do you speak French?
Est-ce que votre ami est jeune? Is your friend young?

b) When the subject of the verb is a pronoun, the subject may be placed after the verb:

Vous parlez français?
Parlez-vous français? } Do you speak French?

c) When the subject is a noun, the noun stands before the verb and a corresponding pronoun is placed after the verb:

Votre ami est-il jeune? Is your friend young?

d) **–t–** is added for euphony when a third-person verb ends in a vowel and the following pronoun-subject begins with a vowel:

Y a-t-il un remède? Is there a cure for it?

24. Relative Pronouns

a) **qui** who, which (*subject*)
que whom, which (*direct object*)
dont of whom, of which

l'homme qui parle	the man who is speaking
les dames que vous voyez	the ladies (whom) you see
le pays dont je parle	the country of which I speak

b) **Lequel,** in its appropriate form, is used after prepositions in reference to things:

les plumes avec lesquelles j'écris	the pens with which I write

c) **ce qui, ce que** = *that which, what*

Faites ce qui est juste. Do what (that which) is right.

25. Interrogative Adjectives and Pronouns

a) Adjectives

	SINGULAR		PLURAL	
Masc.	**quel**	what? which?	**quels**	what? which?
Fem.	**quelle**		**quelles**	

Quel livre aimez-vous?	Which book do you like?
Quelles sont vos raisons?	What are your reasons?

Quel is also used in exclamations:

quelle belle femme! what (a) beautiful woman!

b) Pronouns

Referring to persons	**qui** *or* **qui est-ce qui?**	who?
	qui *or* **qui est-ce que?**	whom?
Referring to things	**qu'est-ce qui?**	what? (*subject*)
	que *or* **qu'est-ce que?**	what? (*direct object*)
	quoi?	what? (*after preposition*)

Qui est là?	Who is there?
Qu'est-ce qui est arrivé?	What happened?
Que faites-vous?	What are you doing?
De quoi parlez-vous?	What are you speaking of?

26. Tenses of the Verb (that differ from English)

a) The present indicative is often used for a future to indicate definite or immediate action:

Je pars demain. I (shall) leave tomorrow.

The present indicative is used to indicate an action begun in the past and still going on:

Il est malade depuis deux jours. He has been ill for two days.

b) The imperfect indicative is used to describe a state or condition, a continued or customary act:

Il écrivait quand je suis entré.	He was writing when I entered.
A Paris je dînais à huit heures.	In Paris I used to dine at eight o'clock.

c) The perfect indicative expresses completed action in the past:

Hier j'ai dîné à huit heures.	Yesterday I dined at eight o'clock.

d) The future is used when future time is implied after **quand, lorsque,** *when;* **dès que, aussitôt que,** *as soon as:*

Je le verrai quand il arrivera.	I'll see him when he arrives.

27. The subjunctive is used principally

a) When the main clause expresses volition, emotion, doubt, etc.:

Il veut que je fasse cela.	He wants me to do that.
Je crains qu'il soit malade.	I am afraid he is ill.

b) After certain impersonal expressions, such as **il faut, il est nécessaire, il est possible,** etc.:

Il faut que j'y aille.	I must go there.
BUT: **Il est certain que j'y irai.**	It is certain that I'll go there.

c) After certain locutions such as **afin que, pour que,** *so that, in order that;* **à moins que,** *unless;* **avant que,** *before;* **bien que,** *although, even though:*

Je partirai bien qu'il fasse mauvais temps.	I shall leave even though the weather is bad.

d) In a relative clause that refers to an indefinite or negative antecedent:

Nous cherchons quelqu'un qui puisse se charger de la correspondance.	We are looking for someone who can take care of our correspondence.
Je ne connais personne qui sache le russe.	I don't know anybody who knows Russian.

28. When the main verb and the subordinate verb have the same subject, the infinitive is generally used instead of a subjunctive clause:

Je regrette d'être en retard.	I am sorry I am late.

29. The infinitive is used instead of the English present participle

a) After a preposition, except **en:**

Il est parti sans me voir.	He left without seeing me.

b) After **voir, entendre,** etc.:

Je l'ai vu venir.	I saw him coming.
Entendez-vous chanter?	Do you hear singing?

30. *a*) The true passive voice is formed with the verb **être** and the past participle, the agent being usually expressed by **par:**

Il a été guéri par ce médecin.	He was cured by this doctor.

b) In conversation the true passive is frequently replaced by the active form with **on** as subject when the agent is not expressed:

Ici on parle anglais.	English is spoken here.
On a arrêté le voleur.	The thief was caught.

c) If the subject is a thing or an idea, the verb is often reflexive:

Le livre se vend ici.	The book is sold here.
Cela se comprend.	That is understood.

31. Cardinal Numbers

1 un, une
2 deux
3 trois
4 quatre
5 cinq
6 six
7 sept
8 huit
9 neuf
10 dix
11 onze
12 douze
13 treize
14 quatorze
15 quinze
16 seize
17 dix-sept
18 dix-huit
19 dix-neuf
20 vingt
21 vingt et un(e)
22 vingt-deux
23 vingt-trois, etc.
30 trente
31 trente et un(e)
32 trente-deux, etc.
40 quarante
41 quarante et un(e)
42 quarante-deux, etc.
50 cinquante
51 cinquante et un(e)
52 cinquante-deux, etc.
60 soixante
61 soixante et un(e)
62 soixante-deux, etc.
70 soixante-dix
71 soixante et onze
72 soixante-douze
73 soixante-treize
74 soixante-quatorze
75 soixante-quinze
76 soixante-seize
77 soixante-dix-sept
78 soixante-dix-huit
79 soixante-dix-neuf
80 quatre-vingts
81 quatre-vingt-un(e)
82 quatre-vingt-deux, etc.
90 quatre-vingt-dix
91 quatre-vingt-onze
92 quatre-vingt-douze
93 quatre-vingt-treize

94 quatre-vingt-quatorze
95 quatre-vingt-quinze
96 quatre-vingt-seize
97 quatre-vingt-dix-sept
98 quatre-vingt-dix-huit
99 quatre-vingt-dix-neuf
100 cent
101 cent un
102 cent deux, etc.

200 deux cents
1000 mille
1001 mille un
1002 mille deux, etc.
1500 mille cinq cents *or* quinze cents
2000 deux mille
1,000,000 un million

32.

1 centimètre = .393 inches
1 mètre = 39.37 inches or 3.28 feet or 1.093 yards
1 kilomètre (km) = .621 miles
1 litre = 2.113 pints or 1.056 quarts or .264 gallons
1 gramme = .035 ounces
1 kilogramme (kilo) = 2.204 pounds or 35.273 ounces
1 livre (demi-kilo) = half a kilogram

0° centigrade = 32 degrees Fahrenheit
100° C = 180° F
1° C = 1.8°F

To change degrees F to degrees C, subtract 32 and multiply by $\frac{5}{9}$. $(F - 32) \times \frac{5}{9} = C$

To change degrees C to degrees F, multiply by $\frac{9}{5}$ and add 32. $(C \times \frac{9}{5}) + 32 = F$

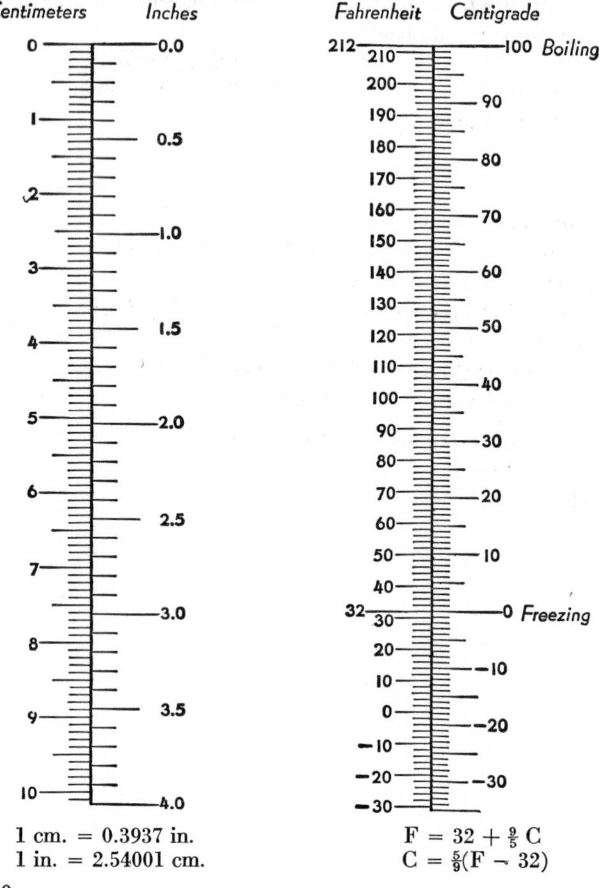

1 cm. = 0.3937 in.
1 in. = 2.54001 cm.

$F = 32 + \frac{9}{5} C$
$C = \frac{5}{9}(F - 32)$

33. A few place names and their derivative adjectives. (The English equivalent is omitted when the meaning is apparent.)

Algérie *f.*	algérien, –ne
Allemagne *f.* (*Germany*)	allemand, –e (*German*)
Angleterre *f.*	anglais, –e
Argentine *f.*	argentin, –e
Autriche *f.*	autrichien, –ne
Belgique *f.*	belge
Brésil *m.*	brésilien, –ne
Canada *m.*	canadien, –ne
Chili *m.*	chilien, –ne
Chine *f.*	chinois, –e
Écosse *f.*	écossais, –e
Égypte *f.*	égyptien, –ne
Espagne *f.*	espagnol, –e
Europe *f.*	européen, –ne
France *f.*	français, –e
Grèce *f.*	grec, grecque
Hollande *f.*	hollandais, –e
Irlande *f.*	irlandais, –e
Italie *f.*	italien, –ne
Japon *m.*	japonais, –e
Maroc *m.*	marocain, –e
Mexique *m.*	mexicain, –e
Norvège *f.*	norvégien, –ne
Péru *m.*	péruvien, –ne
Pologne *f.*	polonais, –e
Portugal *m.*	portugais, –e
Roumanie *f.*	roumain, –e
Russie *f.*	russe
Suède *f.*	suédois, –e
Suisse *f.*	suisse

Tchécoslovaquie *f.*	tchécoslovaque
Turquie *f.*	turc, turcque
Yougoslavie *f.*	yougoslave

34. Conjugation of the Verbs **avoir** and **être**

avoir *to have*	**être** *to be*

INDICATIVE MOOD

Present

I have, am having, do have, etc.	*I am, am being, etc.*
j'ai	je suis
tu as	tu es
il a	il est
nous avons	nous sommes
vous avez	vous êtes
ils ont	ils sont

Imperfect

I was having, used to have, had, etc.	*I was being, used to be, was, etc.*
j'avais	j'étais
tu avais	tu étais
il avait	il était
nous avions	nous étions
vous aviez	vous étiez
ils avaient	ils étaient

Past Definite

I had, etc.	*I was, etc.*
j'eus	je fus
tu eus	tu fus
il eut	il fut
nous eûmes	nous fûmes
vous eûtes	vous fûtes
ils eurent	ils furent

Past Indefinite

I have had, had, did have, etc.	*I have been, was, etc.*
j'ai eu	j'ai été
tu as eu	tu as été
il a eu	il a été
nous avons eu	nous avons été
vous avez eu	vous avez été
ils ont eu	ils ont été

Pluperfect

I had had, etc.	*I had been, etc.*
j'avais eu	j'avais été
tu avais eu	tu avais été
il avait eu	il avait été
nous avions eu	nous avions été
vous aviez eu	vous aviez été
ils avaient eu	ils avaient été

Past Anterior

I had had, etc.	*I had been, etc.*
j'eus eu	j'eus été
tu eus eu	tu eus été
il eut eu	il eut été
nous eûmes eu	nous eûmes été
vous eûtes eu	vous eûtes été
ils eurent eu	ils eurent été

Future

I shall have, etc.	*I shall be, etc.*
j'aurai	je serai
tu auras	tu seras
il aura	il sera
nous aurons	nous serons
vous aurez	vous serez
ils auront	ils seront

Conditional

I should have, etc.	*I should be, etc.*
j'aurais	je serais
tu aurais	tu serais
il aurait	il serait
nous aurions	nous serions
vous auriez	vous seriez
ils auraient	ils seraient

Future Perfect

I shall have had, etc.	*I shall have been, etc.*
j'aurai eu	j'aurai été
tu auras eu	tu auras été
il aura eu	il aura été
nous aurons eu	nous aurons été
vous aurez eu	vous aurez été
ils auront eu	ils auront été

Conditional Perfect

I should have had, etc.	*I should have been, etc.*
j'aurais eu	j'aurais été
tu aurais eu	tu aurais été
il aurait eu	il aurait été
nous aurions eu	nous aurions été
vous auriez eu	vous auriez été
ils auraient eu	ils auraient été

SUBJUNCTIVE MOOD

Present

that I (may) have, etc.	*that I (may) be, etc.*
que j'aie	que je sois
que tu aies	que tu sois
qu'il ait	qu'il soit
que nous ayons	que nous soyons
que vous ayez	que vous soyez
qu'ils aient	qu'ils soient

Imperfect

that I might have, etc.	*that I might be, etc.*
que j'eusse	que je fusse
que tu eusses	que tu fusses
qu'il eût	qu'il fût
que nous eussions	que nous fussions
que vous eussiez	que vous fussiez
qu'ils eussent	qu'ils fussent

Perfect

that I (may) have had, etc.	*that I (may) have been, etc.*
que j'aie eu	que j'aie été
que tu aies eu	que tu aies été
qu'il ait eu	qu'il ait été
que nous ayons eu	que nous ayons été
que vous ayez eu	que vous ayez été
qu'ils aient eu	qu'ils aient été

Pluperfect

that I might have had, etc.	*that I might have been, etc.*
que j'eusse eu	que j'eusse été
que tu eusses eu	que tu eusses été
qu'il eût eu	qu'il eût été
que nous eussions eu	que nous eussions été
que vous eussiez eu	que vous eussiez été
qu'ils eussent eu	qu'ils eussent été

IMPERATIVE

——	ayons, *let us have*	——	soyons, *let us be*
aie, *have (thou)*	ayez, *have (you)*	sois, *be (thou)*	soyez, *be (you)*

35. Regular Verbs: three conjugations

I	II	III
	Infinitive	
parler, *to speak*	**finir,** *to finish*	**entendre,** *to hear*

Present Participle

parlant, *speaking*	finissant, *finishing*	entendant, *hearing*

Past Participle

parlé, *spoken*	fini, *finished*	entendu, *heard*

INDICATIVE MOOD

Present

I speak, am speaking, etc.	*I finish, am finishing, etc.*	*I hear, am hearing, etc.*
je parle	je finis	j'entends
tu parles	tu finis	tu entends
il parle	il finit	il entend
nous parlons	nous finissons	nous entendons
vous parlez	vous finissez	vous entendez
ils parlent	ils finissent	ils entendent

Imperfect

I was speaking, used to speak, etc.	*I was finishing, used to finish, etc.*	*I was hearing, used to hear, etc.*
je parlais	je finissais	j'entendais
tu parlais	tu finissais	tu entendais
il parlait	il finissait	il entendait
nous parlions	nous finissions	nous entendions
vous parliez	vous finissiez	vous entendiez
ils parlaient	ils finissaient	ils entendaient

Past Definite

I spoke, etc.	*I finished, etc.*	*I heard, etc.*
je parlai	je finis	j'entendis
tu parlas	tu finis	tu entendis
il parla	il finit	il entendit
nous parlâmes	nous finîmes	nous entendîmes
vous parlâtes	vous finîtes	vous entendîtes
ils parlèrent	ils finirent	ils entendirent

Past Indefinite

I spoke, have spoken, etc.	*I finished, have finished, etc.*	*I heard, have heard, etc.*
j'ai parlé	j'ai fini	j'ai entendu
tu as parlé	tu as fini	tu as entendu
il a parlé	il a fini	il a entendu
nous avons parlé	nous avons fini	nous avons entendu
vous avez parlé	vous avez fini	vous avez entendu
ils ont parlé	ils ont fini	ils ont entendu

Pluperfect

I had spoken, etc.	*I had finished, etc.*	*I had heard, etc.*
j'avais parlé	j'avais fini	j'avais entendu
tu avais parlé	tu avais fini	tu avais entendu
il avait parlé	il avait fini	il avait entendu
nous avions parlé	nous avions fini	nous avions entendu
vous aviez parlé	vous aviez fini	vous aviez entendu
ils avaient parlé	ils avaient fini	ils avaient entendu

Past Anterior

I had spoken, etc.	*I had finished, etc.*	*I had heard, etc.*
j'eus parlé	j'eus fini	j'eus entendu
tu eus parlé	tu eus fini	tu eus entendu
il eut parlé	il eut fini	il eut entendu
nous eûmes parlé	nous eûmes fini	nous eûmes entendu
vous eûtes parlé	vous eûtes fini	vous eûtes entendu
ils eurent parlé	ils eurent fini	ils eurent entendu

Future

I shall speak, etc.	*I shall finish, etc.*	*I shall hear, etc.*
je parlerai	je finirai	j'entendrai
tu parleras	tu finiras	tu entendras
il parlera	il finira	il entendra
nous parlerons	nous finirons	nous entendrons
vous parlerez	vous finirez	vous entendrez
ils parleront	ils finiront	ils entendront

Conditional

I should speak, etc.	*I should finish, etc.*	*I should hear, etc.*
je parlerais	je finirais	j'entendrais
tu parlerais	tu finirais	tu entendrais
il parlerait	il finirait	il entendrait
nous parlerions	nous finirions	nous entendrions
vous parleriez	vous finiriez	vous entendriez
ils parleraient	ils finiraient	ils entendraient

Future Perfect

I shall have spoken, etc.	*I shall have finished, etc.*	*I shall have heard, etc.*
j'aurai parlé	j'aurai fini	j'aurai entendu
tu auras parlé	tu auras fini	tu auras entendu
il aura parlé	il aura fini	il aura entendu
nous aurons parlé	nous aurons fini	nous aurons entendu
vous aurez parlé	vous aurez fini	vous aurez entendu
ils auront parlé	ils auront fini	ils auront entendu

Conditional Perfect

I should have spoken, etc.	*I should have finished, etc.*	*I should have heard, etc.*
j'aurais parlé	j'aurais fini	j'aurais entendu
tu aurais parlé	tu aurais fini	tu aurais entendu
il aurait parlé	il aurait fini	il aurait entendu
nous aurions parlé	nous aurions fini	nous aurions entendu
vous auriez parlé	vous auriez fini	vous auriez entendu
ils auraient parlé	ils auraient fini	ils auraient entendu

SUBJUNCTIVE MOOD

Present

that I (may) speak, etc.	*that I (may) finish, etc.*	*that I (may) hear, etc.*
que je parle	que je finisse	que j'entende
que tu parles	que tu finisses	que tu entendes
qu'il parle	qu'il finisse	qu'il entende
que nous parlions	que nous finissions	que nous entendions
que vous parliez	que vous finissiez	que vous entendiez
qu'ils parlent	qu'ils finissent	qu'ils entendent

IMPERFECT

that I (might) speak, etc.	*that I (might) finish, etc.*	*that I (might) hear, etc.*
que je parlasse	que je finisse	que j'entendisse
que tu parlasses	que tu finisses	que tu entendisses
qu'il parlât	qu'il finît	qu'il entendît
que nous parlassions	que nous finissions	que nous entendissions
que vous parlassiez	que vous finissiez	que vous entendissiez
qu'ils parlassent	qu'ils finissent	qu'ils entendissent

PERFECT

that I (may) have spoken, etc.	*that I (may) have finished, etc.*	*that I (may) have heard, etc.*
que j'aie parlé	que j'aie fini	que j'aie entendu
que tu aies parlé	que tu aies fini	que tu aies entendu
qu'il ait parlé	qu'il ait fini	qu'il ait entendu
que nous ayons parlé	que nous ayons fini	que nous ayons entendu
que vous ayez parlé	que vous ayez fini	que vous ayez entendu
qu'ils aient parlé	qu'ils aient fini	qu'ils aient entendu

PLUPERFECT

that I (might) have spoken, etc.	*that I (might) have finished, etc.*	*that I (might) have heard, etc.*
que j'eusse parlé	que j'eusse fini	que j'eusse entendu
que tu eusses parlé	que tu eusses fini	que tu eusses entendu
qu'il eût parlé	qu'il eût fini	qu'il eût entendu
nous eussions parlé [1]	nous eussions fini [1]	nous eussions entendu [1]
vous eussiez parlé	vous eussiez fini	vous eussiez entendu
ils eussent parlé	ils eussent fini	ils eussent entendu

IMPERATIVE

parle, *speak*	finis, *finish*	entends, *hear*
parlons, *let us speak*	finissons, *let us finish*	entendons, *let us hear*
parlez, *speak*	finissez, *finish*	entendez, *hear*

[1] **Que** has been omitted to save space, but it should be used in conjugating these forms.

36. The Passive Voice

INFINITIVES

PRESENT	PAST
être aimé(e)(s), *to be loved*	**avoir été aimé(e)(s),** *to have been loved*

PARTICIPLES

PRESENT	PAST
étant aimé(e)(s), *being loved*	**ayant été aimé(e)(s),** *having been loved*

INDICATIVE MOOD

PRESENT	PAST INDEFINITE
I am (being) loved, etc.	*I have been (was) loved, etc.*
je suis aimé(e)	**j'ai été aimé(e)**
tu es aimé(e)	**tu as été aimé(e)**
il (elle) est aimé(e)	**il (elle) a été aimé(e)**
nous sommes aimé(e)s	**nous avons été aimé(e)s**
vous êtes aimé(e)s	**vous avez été aimé(e)s**
ils (elles) sont aimé(e)s	**ils (elles) ont été aimé(e)s**

IMPERFECT	PLUPERFECT
I was (being) loved, etc.	*I had been loved, etc.*
j'étais aimé(e), etc.	**j'avais été aimé(e), etc.**

PAST DEFINITE	PAST ANTERIOR
I was loved, etc.	*I had been loved, etc.*
je fus aimé(e), etc.	**j'eus été aimé(e), etc.**

FUTURE	FUTURE PERFECT
I shall be loved, etc.	*I shall have been loved, etc.*
je serai aimé(e), etc.	**j'aurai été aimé(e), etc.**

CONDITIONAL	CONDITIONAL PERFECT
I should be loved, etc.	*I should have been loved, etc.*
je serais aimé(e), etc.	**j'aurais été aimé(e), etc.**

SUBJUNCTIVE MOOD

PRESENT	PERFECT
that I (may) be loved, etc.	*that I (may) have been loved, etc.*
que je sois aimé(e), etc.	que j'aie été aimé(e), etc.
IMPERFECT	PLUPERFECT
that I (might) be loved, etc.	*that I (might) have been loved, etc.*
que je fusse aimé(e), etc.	que j'eusse été aimé(e), etc.

IMPERATIVE

sois aimé(e), *be loved*
soyons aimé(e)s, *let us be loved*
soyez aimé(e)s, *be loved*

37. The Reflexive Verb

INFINITIVES

PRESENT	PAST
se laver, *to wash oneself*	s'être lavé(e)(s), *to have washed oneself*

PARTICIPLES

PRESENT	PAST
se lavant, *washing oneself*	s'étant lavé(e)(s), *having washed oneself*

INDICATIVE MOOD

PRESENT	PAST INDEFINITE
I wash (am washing) myself, etc.	*I washed (have washed) myself, etc.*
je me lave	je me suis lavé(e)
tu te laves	tu t'es lavé(e)
il se lave	il (elle) s'est lavé(e)
nous nous lavons	nous nous sommes lavé(e)s
vous vous lavez	vous vous êtes lavé(e)s
ils se lavent	ils (elles) se sont lavé(e)s

IMPERFECT

I was washing (washed) myself, etc.

je me lavais, etc.

PLUPERFECT

I had washed myself, etc.

je m'étais lavé(e), etc.

PAST DEFINITE

I washed myself, etc.

je me lavai, etc.

PAST ANTERIOR

I had washed myself, etc.

je me fus lavé(e), etc.

FUTURE

I shall wash myself, etc.

je me laverai, etc.

FUTURE PERFECT

I shall have washed myself, etc.

je me serai lavé(e), etc.

CONDITIONAL

I should wash myself, etc.

je me laverais, etc.

CONDITIONAL PERFECT

I should have washed myself, etc.

je me serais lavé(e), etc.

SUBJUNCTIVE MOOD

PRESENT

that I (may) wash myself, etc.

que je me lave, etc.

PAST

that I (may) have washed myself, etc.

que je me sois lavé(e), etc.

IMPERFECT

that I (might) wash myself, etc.

que je me lavasse, etc.

PLUPERFECT

that I (might) have washed myself, etc.

que je me fusse lavé(e), etc.

IMPERATIVE

lave-toi, *wash thyself (yourself)*
lavons-nous, *let us wash ourselves*
lavez-vous, *wash yourselves (yourself)*

38. Verbs in –**ier**, –**ouer**, and –**uer**

The vowels **i, ou, u** lose their full vowel value before a pronounced vowel and become semi-vowels, but they retain the full vowel value before a mute **e.**

copier, *to copy*	**jouer,** *to play*	**continuer,** *to continue*
	PRESENT	
je copie [kɔpi]	joue [ʒu]	continue [kɔ̃tiny]
tu copies [kɔpi]	joues [ʒu]	continues [kɔ̃tiny]
il copie [kɔpi]	joue [ʒu]	continue [kɔ̃tiny]
nous copions [kɔpjɔ̃]	jouons [ʒwɔ̃]	continuons [kɔ̃tinɥɔ̃]
vous copiez [kɔpje]	jouez [ʒwe]	continuez [kɔ̃tinɥe]
ils copient [kɔpi]	jouent [ʒu]	continuent [kɔ̃tiny]
	IMPERFECT	
je copiais [kɔpjɛ] etc.	jouais [ʒwɛ] etc.	continuais [kɔ̃tinɥɛ] etc.
	FUTURE	
je copierai [kɔpire] etc.	jouerai [ʒure] etc.	continuerai [kɔ̃tinyre] etc.
	CONDITIONAL	
je copierais [kɔpirɛ] etc.	jouerais [ʒurɛ] etc.	continuerais [kɔ̃tinyrɛ] etc.
	PAST PARTICIPLE	
copié [kɔpje]	joué [ʒwe]	continué [kɔ̃tinɥe]

39. Orthographic (Spelling) Changes in Verbs

1. Verbs ending in –**cer,** *e.g.* **avancer** [avɑ̃se], *advance,* must preserve the [s] sound of **c** throughout their conjugation, and hence **c** becomes **ç** when it precedes **a** or **o** of an ending, but not elsewhere.

PRES. PART.	PRES. INDIC.	IMPF. INDIC.	PAST DEF.	IMPF. SUBJ.
avançant	avance	avançais	avançai	avançasse
	avances	avançais	avanças	avançasses
	avance	avançait	avança	avançât
	avançons	avancions	avançâmes	avançassions
	avancez	avanciez	avançâtes	avançassiez
	avancent	avançaient	avancèrent	avançassent

NOTE. Pronoun subjects are omitted to save space.

2. Verbs ending in **–ger,** *e.g.* **manger** [mɑ̃ʒe], *eat,* must preserve the [ʒ] sound of **g** throughout their conjugation, and hence **g** becomes **ge** when it precedes **a** or **o** of an ending, but not elsewhere.

Pres. Part.	Pres. Indic.	Impf. Indic.	Past Def.	Impf. Subj.
mangeant	mange	mangeais	mangeai	mangeasse
	manges	mangeais	mangeas	mangeasses
	mange	mangeait	mangea	mangeât
	mangeons	mangions	mangeâmes	mangeassions
	mangez	mangiez	mangeâtes	mangeassiez
	mangent	mangeaient	mangèrent	mangeassent

3. Verbs ending in **–oyer** and **–uyer,** *e.g.* **nettoyer,** *clean,* **essuyer,** *wipe,* change **y** to **i** whenever it comes before **e** mute in conjugation, but not elsewhere; verbs in **–ayer,** *e.g.* **payer,** *pay,* may retain **y** throughout, or change **y** to **i** before **e** mute.

Pres. Indic.	Pres. Subj.	Future	Conditional
nettoie	nettoie	nettoierai	nettoierais
nettoies	nettoies	nettoieras	nettoierais
nettoie	nettoie	nettoiera	nettoierait
nettoyons	nettoyions	nettoierons	nettoierions
nettoyez	nettoyiez	nettoierez	nettoieriez
nettoient	nettoient	nettoieront	nettoieraient
essuie etc.	essuie etc.	essuierai etc.	essuierais etc.
paie / paye } etc.	paie / paye } etc.	paierai / payerai } etc.	paierais / payerais } etc.

4. Verbs having the stem vowel **e,** *e.g.* **mener,** *lead,* change this **e** to **è** wherever in conjugating the verb it is followed by a syllable containing **e** mute (but for verbs in **–eler, –eter,** see the next page).

Pres. Indic.	**Pres. Subj.**	**Future**	**Conditional**
mène	mène	mènerai	mènerais
mènes	mènes	mèneras	mènerais
mène	mène	mènera	mènerait
menons	menions	mènerons	mènerions
menez	meniez	mènerez	mèneriez
mènent	mènent	mèneront	mèneraient

5. Verbs having the stem vowel **é** followed by a consonant, *e.g.* **céder**, *yield*, change **é** to **è** in the present indicative and subjunctive, but retain **é** in the future and conditional when followed by a syllable containing **e** mute.

Pres. Indic.	Pres. Subj.	Future	Conditional
cède, etc.	cède, etc.	céderai, etc.	céderais, etc.

Note. Verbs with stem vowel é + vowel are regular, *e.g.* **créer.**

6. Verbs in **–eler, –eter,** *e.g.* **appeler,** *call*, **jeter,** *throw*, usually double **l** or **t** before an **e** mute syllable in conjugation (but for some important exceptions, see below).

Pres. Indic.	Pres. Subj.	Future	Conditional
appelle	appelle	appellerai	appellerais
appelles	appelles	appelleras	appellerais
appelle	appelle	appellera	appellerait
appelons	appelions	appellerons	appellerions
appelez	appeliez	appellerez	appelleriez
appellent	appellent	appelleront	appelleraient
So also **jeter:**			
jette, etc.	jette, etc.	jetterai, etc.	jetterais, etc.

7. A few verbs in **–eler, –eter** (the commonest being **geler,** *freeze*, **acheter,** *buy*) take the grave accent like **mener.**

Pres. Indic.	Pres. Subj.	Future	Conditional
gèle, etc.	gèle, etc.	gèlerai, etc.	gèlerais, etc.
achète, etc.	achète, etc.	achèterai, etc.	achèterais, etc.

40. List of the Principal Irregular Verbs

Infinitive	Participles	Present Indicative	
acquérir, *to acquire*	**acquérant** **acquis, -e**	**j'acquiers** tu acquiers il acquiert	nous acquérons vous acquérez ils acquièrent
aller, *to go*	**allant** **allé, -e**	**je vais** tu vas il va	nous allons vous allez ils vont
s'asseoir, *to sit down*	**s'asseyant** [1] **assis, -e**	**je m'assieds** tu t'assieds il s'assied	nous nous asseyons vous vous asseyez ils s'asseyent [2]
avoir, *to have*	**ayant** **eu, -e**	**j'ai** tu as il a	nous avons vous avez ils ont
battre, *to beat*	**battant** **battu, -e**	**je bats** tu bats il bat	nous battons vous battez ils battent
boire, *to drink*	**buvant** **bu, -e**	**je bois** tu bois il boit	nous buvons vous buvez ils boivent
conduire, *to conduct*	**conduisant** **conduit, -e**	**je conduis** tu conduis il conduit	nous conduisons vous conduisez ils conduisent
connaître, *to know*	**connaissant** **connu, -e**	**je connais** tu connais il connaît	nous connaissons vous connaissez ils connaissent

[1] *Or* s'assoyant. [2] *Or* je m'assois, tu t'assois, il s'assoit, nous nous assoyons, vous vous assoyez, ils s'assoient.

Past Definite	Future	Present Subjunctive	Imperative
j'acquis	j'acquerrai	que j'acquière que nous acquérions qu'ils acquièrent	acquiers acquérons acquérez
j'allai	j'irai	que j'aille que nous allions qu'ils aillent	va allons allez
je m'assis	je m'assiérai (asseyerai) (assoirai)	que je m'asseye nous nous asseyions [3] qu'ils s'asseyent [4]	assieds-toi asseyons-nous asseyez-vous [5]
j'eus	j'aurai	que j'aie que nous ayons qu'ils aient	aie ayons ayez
je battis	je battrai	que je batte que nous battions qu'ils battent	bats battons battez
je bus	je boirai	que je boive que nous buvions qu'ils boivent	bois buvons buvez
je conduisis	je conduirai	que je conduise que nous conduisions qu'ils conduisent	conduis conduisons conduisez
je connus	je connaîtrai	que je connaisse que nous connaissions qu'ils connaissent	connais connaissons connaissez

[3] See note 1, page 199. [4] *Or* que je m'assoie, que nous nous assoyions, qu'ils s'assoient. [5] *Or* assois-toi, assoyons-nous, assoyez-vous.

Infinitive	Participles	Present Indicative	
construire, *to construct,* is conjugated like **conduire**			
coudre, *to sew*	**cousant** **cousu, –e**	**je couds** tu couds il coud	nous cousons vous cousez ils cousent
courir, *to run*	**courant** **couru**	**je cours** tu cours il court	nous courons vous courez ils courent
couvrir, *to cover*	**couvrant** **couvert, –e**	**je couvre** tu couvres il couvre	nous couvrons vous couvrez ils couvrent
craindre, *to fear*	**craignant** **craint, –e**	**je crains** tu crains il craint	nous craignons vous craignez ils craignent
croire, *to believe*	**croyant** **cru, –e**	**je crois** tu crois il croit	nous croyons vous croyez ils croient
devoir, *to owe, must*	**devant** **dû,** due	**je dois** tu dois il doit	nous devons vous devez ils doivent
dire, *to say*	**disant** **dit, –e**	**je dis** tu dis il dit	nous disons vous dites ils disent
dormir, *to sleep*	**dormant** **dormi**	**je dors** tu dors il dort	nous dormons vous dormez ils dorment

Past Definite	Future	Present Subjunctive	Imperative
je cousis	je coudrai	que je couse	couds cousons cousez
je courus	je courrai	que je coure que nous courions qu'ils courent	cours courons courez
je couvris	je couvrirai	que je couvre que nous couvrions qu'ils couvrent	couvre couvrons couvrez
je craignis	je craindrai	que je craigne que nous craignions qu'ils craignent	crains craignons craignez
je crus	je croirai	que je croie que nous croyions qu'ils croient	crois croyons croyez
je dus	je devrai	que je doive que nous devions qu'ils doivent	dois devons devez
je dis	je dirai	que je dise que nous disions qu'ils disent	dis disons dites
je dormis	je dormirai	que je dorme que nous dormions qu'ils dorment	dors dormons dormez

Infinitive	Participles	Present Indicative	
écrire, *to write*	**écrivant** **écrit, –e**	**j'écris** tu écris il écrit	nous écrivons vous écrivez ils écrivent
envoyer, *to send*	**envoyant** **envoyé, –e**	**j'envoie** tu envoies il envoie	nous envoyons vous envoyez ils envoient
être, *to be*	**étant** **été**	**je suis** tu es il est	nous sommes vous êtes ils sont
faire, *to do*	**faisant** **fait, –e**	**je fais** tu fais il fait	nous faisons vous faites ils font
falloir, *to be necessary*	—— **fallu**	**il faut**	
lire, *to read*	**lisant** **lu, –e**	**je lis** tu lis il lit	nous lisons vous lisez ils lisent
mettre, *to put*	**mettant** **mis, –e**	**je mets** tu mets il met	nous mettons vous mettez ils mettent
mourir, *to die*	**mourant** **mort, –e**	**je meurs** tu meurs il meurt	nous mourons vous mourez ils meurent

offrir, *to offer,* conjugated like **couvrir**

ouvrir, *to open,* conjugated like **couvrir**

Past Definite	Future	Present Subjunctive	Imperative
j'écrivis	j'écrirai	que j'écrive que nous écrivions qu'ils écrivent	écris écrivons écrivez
j'envoyai	j'enverrai	que j'envoie que nous envoyions qu'ils envoient	envoie envoyons envoyez
je fus	je serai (*Impf.*) j'étais	que je sois que nous soyons qu'ils soient	sois soyons soyez
je fis	je ferai	que je fasse que nous fassions qu'ils fassent	fais faisons faites
il fallut	il faudra	qu'il faille	
je lus	je lirai	que je lise que nous lisions qu'ils lisent	lis lisons lisez
je mis	je mettrai	que je mette que nous mettions qu'ils mettent	mets mettons mettez
je mourus	je mourrai	que je meure que nous mourions qu'ils meurent	meurs mourons mourez

Infinitive	Participles	Present Indicative	
paraître, *to appear*, conjugated like **connaître**			
partir, *to set out*	**partant** **parti,** –e	conjugated like **dormir**	
plaire, *to please*	**plaisant** **plu**	**je plais** tu plais il plaît	nous plaisons vous plaisez ils plaisent
pleuvoir, *to rain*	**pleuvant** **plu**	**il pleut**	
pouvoir, *to be able*	**pouvant** **pu**	**je peux** (**puis**) tu peux il peut	nous pouvons vous pouvez ils peuvent
prendre, *to take*	**prenant** **pris,** –e	**je prends** tu prends il prend	nous prenons vous prenez ils prennent
recevoir, *to receive*	**recevant** **reçu,** –e	**je reçois** tu reçois il reçoit	nous recevons vous recevez ils reçoivent
rire, *to laugh*	**riant** **ri**	**je ris** tu ris il rit	nous rions vous riez ils rient
savoir, *to know*	**sachant** **su,** –e	**je sais** tu sais il sait	nous savons vous savez ils savent
sentir, *to feel*	**sentant** **senti,** –e	**je sens** conjugated like **dormir**	

Past Definite	Future	Present Subjunctive	Imperative
je plus	je plairai	que je plaise	plais plaisons plaisez
il plut	il pleuvra	qu'il pleuve	
je pus	je pourrai	que je puisse que nous puissions qu'ils puissent	——
je pris	je prendrai	que je prenne que nous prenions qu'ils prennent	prends prenons prenez
je reçus	je recevrai	que je reçoive que nous recevions qu'ils reçoivent	reçois recevons recevez
je ris	je rirai	que je rie que nous riions qu'ils rient	ris rions riez
je sus	je saurai	que je sache que nous sachions qu'ils sachent	sache sachons sachez
je sentis			

Infinitive	Participles	Present Indicative	
servir, *to serve*	**servant** **servi,** –e	**je sers** conjugated like **dormir**	
sortir, *to go out*	**sortant** **sorti,** –e	**je sors** conjugated like **dormir**	
souffrir, *to suffer*	**souffrant** **souffert,** –e	**je souffre** conjugated like **couvrir**	
suivre, *to follow*	**suivant** **suivi,** –e	**je suis** tu suis il suit	nous suivons vous suivez ils suivent
tenir, *to hold*	**tenant** **tenu,** –e	**je tiens** tu tiens il tient	nous tenons vous tenez ils tiennent
venir, *to come*	**venant** **venu,** –e	**je viens** conjugated like **tenir**	
voir, *to see*	**voyant** **vu,** –e	**je vois** tu vois il voit	nous voyons vous voyez ils voient
vouloir, *to be willing*	**voulant** **voulu,** –e	**je veux** tu veux il veut	nous voulons vous voulez ils veulent

Past Definite	Future	Present Subjunctive	Imperative
je servis			
je sortis			
je souffris			
je suivis	je suivrai	que je suive que nous suivions qu'ils suivent	suis suivons suivez
je tins nous tînmes ils tinrent	je tiendrai	que je tienne que nous tenions qu'ils tiennent	tiens tenons tenez
je vins			
je vis	je verrai	que je voie que nous voyions qu'ils voient	vois voyons voyez
je voulus	je voudrai	que je veuille que nous voulions qu'ils veuillent	veuille veuillons veuillez

41. Aliments et boissons (*Food and drinks*)

CONDIMENT SEASONING

ail *m.* garlic
huile *f.* oil
mayonnaise *f.* mayonnaise
moutarde *f.* mustard
oignon *m.* onion
poivre *m.* pepper
sel *m.* salt
vinaigre *m.* vinegar

PAIN BREAD

biscuit *m.* biscuit
croissant *m.* crescent-shaped bun
croûte *f.* crust
flûte *f.* long thin loaf
galette *f.* pancake
mie *f.* crumb
pain blanc *m.* white bread
pain bis *m.* brown bread
pain frais *m.* fresh bread
pain noir *m.* black bread
pain rassis *m.* stale bread
pain de seigle *m.* rye bread
tranche *f.* slice

HORS-D'ŒUVRE HORS D'OEUVRES

anchois *m.* anchovy
beurre *m.* butter
cornichon *m.* pickle
hareng *m.* herring
olive *f.* olive
radis *m.* radish
sardine *f.* sardine
saucisson *m.* sausage

POTAGE SOUP

bouillon *m.* bouillon
consommé *m.* consommé
potage julienne *m.* vegetable soup
potage parmentier *m.* potato soup
soupe à l'oignon *f.* onion soup

ŒUFS EGGS

œuf à la coque *m.* soft-boiled egg
œuf dur *m.* hard-boiled egg
œufs brouillés *m. pl.* scrambled eggs
œuf sur le plat *m.* fried egg
omelette aux fines herbes *f.* herb omelet
omelette au lard *f.* omelet with bacon

POISSONS ET COQUILLAGES — SEA FOOD

clovisse *f.* clam
crabe *m.* crab
crevette *f.* shrimp
hareng *m.* herring
homard *m.* lobster
huître *f.* oyster
langouste *f.* crayfish
maquereau *m.* mackerel
merlan *m.* whiting
morue *f.* cod
moule *f.* mussel
raie *f.* ray
saumon *m.* salmon
sole *f.* sole
thon *m.* tuna
truite *f.* trout

VIANDES — MEATS

agneau *m.* lamb
aloyau *m.* sirloin
bifteck *m.* beefsteak
bœuf *m.* beef
cervelle *f.* brains
côtelette de mouton *f.* mutton chop
côtelette de veau *f.* veal cutlet
escargot *m.* snail
filet *m.* tenderloin
foie *m.* liver
gigot de mouton *m.* leg of lamb
jambon *m.* ham
langue *f.* tongue
pâté *m.* meat pie
porc *m.* pork
ragoût *m.* stew
ris de veau *m.* sweetbread
rognon *m.* kidney
tripe *f.* tripe
veau *m.* veal

VOLAILLE — FOWL

chapon *m.* capon
dinde *f.* turkey
oie *f.* goose
poulet *m.* chicken
aile *f.* wing
blanc *m.* breast (*of a fowl*)
cuisse *f.* leg

VENAISON — GAME

caille *f.* quail
canard *m.* duck
cerf *m.* deer
chevreuil *m.* roe
faisan *m.* pheasant
lapin *m.* rabbit
lièvre *m.* hare
perdrix *f.* partridge
sanglier *m.* wild boar

LÉGUMES — VEGETABLES

asperges *f. pl.* asparagus
aubergine *f.* egg plant
betterave *f.* beet
carrote *f.* carrot

céleri *m.* celery
chicorée *f.* chicory
chou *m.* cabbage
choux de Bruxelles *m. pl.* Brussels sprouts
chou-fleur *m.* cauliflower
concombre *m.* cucumber
cresson *m.* water cress
endive *f.* endive
épinards *m. pl.* spinach
haricots *m. pl.* beans
haricots verts *m. pl.* string beans
laitue *f.* lettuce
maïz *m.* sweet corn
navet *m.* turnip
patate *f.* sweet potato
petits pois *m. pl.* green peas
tomate *f.* tomato

DESSERT — DESSERT, SWEETS

amende *f.* almond
banane *f.* banana
compote *f.* stewed fruit
confiture *f.* preserves
flan *m.* custard
fromage *m.* cheese
glace *f.* ice cream
gelée *f.* jelly
marmelade *f.* marmalade
miel *m.* honey
noix *f.* walnut
pâtisserie *f.* pastry
tarte *f.* (fruit) pie

FRUITS — FRUIT

abricot *m.* apricot
ananas *m.* pineapple
avocat *m.* avocado
cerise *f.* cherry
citron *m.* lemon
date *f.* date
figue *f.* fig
fraise *f.* strawberry
framboise *f.* raspberry
grenade *f.* pomegranate
groseille *f.* currant
limon *m.* lime
mandarine *f.* tangerine
melon *m.* melon
orange *f.* orange
peau *f.* skin
pêche *f.* peach
pépin *m.* seed
pomme *f.* apple
poire *f.* pear
prune *f.* plum
pruneau *m.* prune
raisin *m.* grape

BOISSONS — DRINKS

alcool *m.* alcohol
apéritif *m.* apéritif, appetizer
bière *f.* beer
bière blonde *f.* light beer
bière brune *f.* dark beer

cacao *m.* cocoa
café *m.* coffee
champagne *m.* champagne
chocolat *m.* chocolate
cidre *m.* cider
cognac *m.* brandy, cognac
eau (potable) *f.* (drinking) water
eau gazeuse *f.* charged water
eau minérale *f.* mineral water
eau de Seltz *f.* Seltzer water
eau-de-vie *f.* brandy
gin *m.* gin
lait *m.* milk
lait pasteurisé *m.* pasteurized milk
limonade *f.* lemonade
liqueur *f.* liqueur
orangeade *f.* orangeade
Porto *m.* port wine
rafraîchissement *m.* refreshment
rhum *m.* rum
thé *m.* tea
vin *m.* wine
vin blanc *m.* white wine
vin de Bordeaux *m.* Bordeaux wine
vin de Bourgogne *m.* Burgundy wine
vin mousseux *m.* sparkling wine
vin rosé *m.* rose wine
vin rouge *m.* red wine
Xérès *m.* sherry wine